Designing Programs for New Teachers

The California Experience

Ann I. Morey
Diane S. Murphy
Editors

San Diego State University

April 1990

FAR WEST LABORATORY
FOR EDUCATIONAL RESEARCH AND DEVELOPMENT

ERIC CLEARINGHOUSE
ON EDUCATIONAL MANAGEMENT

Design: Far West Laboratory for Educational Research and Development

International Standard Book Number: 0-86552-104-2
Library of Congress Catalog Card Number: 90-81766

Printed in the United States of America, 1990
Far West Laboratory for Educational Research and Development
1855 Folsom Street, San Francisco, California 94103
and
ERIC Clearinghouse on Educational Management
University of Oregon, Eugene, Oregon 97403

No federal funds were used in the printing of this publication.

Far West Laboratory and the University of Oregon are affirmative action, equal opportunity institutions.

This document is published jointly by the Far West Laboratory for Educational Research and Development and by the ERIC Clearinghouse on Educational Management. A portion of the research was supported by federal funds from the U.S. Department of Education, Office of Educational Research and Improvement. The contents of this publication do not necessarily reflect the views or policies of the Department of Education nor does mention of trade names, commercial products, or organizations imply endorsement by the United States Government. Reprint rights are granted with proper credit.

About FWL

Far West Laboratory for Educational Research and Development is located in San Francisco. With primary funding from the U.S. Department of Education, it conducts research, provides technical assistance and training, and offers evaluation support to schools and education agencies. In addition, for 24 years, FWL has been a federally designated regional laboratory with the charge to provide service and support for the public schools in Arizona, California, Nevada, and Utah. Other funding comes from state and private sources, and addresses the entire range of educational concerns — from preschool experiences through adult literacy.

About San Diego State University

The College of Education at San Diego State University is involved in extensive collaborations with public school personnel and university discipline-based faculty to improve the professional preparation of teachers. Its work in this regard has been recognized by several national awards given by the Association for Teacher Educators and the American Association of State Colleges and Universities. San Diego State University and the San Diego public schools are leaders in the development and evaluation of models of assistance for beginning teachers, with six different models currently under further development.

About ERIC

The Educational Resources Information Center (ERIC) is a national information system operated by the U.S. Department of Education. The ERIC Clearinghouse on Educational Management, one of several such units in the system, was established at the University of Oregon in 1966. ERIC serves the education community by disseminating research results and other resource information that can be used in developing more effective educational programs. Research results and journal articles are announced regularly in ERIC's index and abstract bulletins.

Besides processing documents and journal articles, the Clearinghouse prepares bibliographies, literature reviews, monographs, and other interpretive research studies on topics in its educational area.

Table of Contents

Foreword

W. Ann Reynolds
Chancellor
The California State University

WHO can forget his or her first day — indeed, first year — of teaching? Most of us who recall that memorable time were confronted with a task that by today's standards was easy. Not only are today's beginning teachers expected to perform from their first day as seasoned professionals, but they are expected to do it in a classroom setting that has changed a great deal. When I started teaching, most students spoke English; they were reasonably well prepared; they came from a rather homogeneous culture; and I never had to give a passing thought to classroom safety or graffiti in the halls. Even then there was a lot to learn in order to become a good teacher.

Learning to teach competently is a long-term process, involving several stages of development and extending well into the first years of teaching. Unfortunately, until recently, there has been little recognition of beginning teachers as novices who require stable working conditions and professional support if they are to become competent professionals. Beginning teachers have been expected to assume the same responsibilities and perform as well as those teachers who have had many years of classroom experience. Frequently, working conditions and assignments of beginning teachers are not conducive to their professional development or success. Beginning teachers too often become frustrated with classroom management, overwhelmed with paperwork, and feel inadequate and powerless. Faced with these conditions and lack of support, large numbers of teachers leave the profession within their first few years of teaching.

Preparing teachers who have confidence and competence and will remain in the profession requires a long-term, integrated, systematic approach which extends from undergraduate preparation through professional studies and continues during the novice years of teaching. This model of extended teacher preparation recognizes the continuity of the learning process and the developmental stages in becoming a professional teacher. On this learning continuum, programs for beginning teacher support provide for the transition from university student to professional teacher and are the critical link between theory and its application in the classroom.

To put in place an effective extended approach to teacher preparation, universities and school districts must recognize that they need to be a single highly connected and integrated system for educating teachers. There must be articulation between the components of the extended teacher preparation: undergraduate preparation, professional studies and beginning teacher support programs. Where school-university partnerships have been developed for student teaching or school improvement, these partnerships could become the vehicle for framing and implementing beginning teacher support programs. As well, professional educators should be consulted as university faculty define the university teacher preparation curriculum, and university faculty should be involved in building and delivering the beginning teacher support component. This process will not only result in effective beginning teacher support programs, but will provide opportunities for professional teachers and university faculty to learn about current research on teaching, promising instructional practices, conditions contributing to teaching effectiveness, and the challenges schools face when educating an increasingly diverse student population. True professionals have the capacity to learn and grow throughout their careers. Beginning teacher support programs need to build this capacity in the novice teacher. Too often, help for the beginning teacher is directed toward or limited to a narrow range of classroom survival skills. While survival and adjustment may be an important initial aspect of support for beginning teachers, it should not stop there. Beginning teacher programs should improve and expand the beginning teacher's ability to implement a variety of appropriate instructional strategies including cross-cultural education, curriculum development, diagnosing student learning, selecting and developing effective teaching materials, and assuming school leadership roles.

Assisting beginning teachers in their development toward becoming competent professionals is critically important if we are to strengthen K-12 education, particularly for ethnically and linguistically diverse students. We cannot afford to waste our investment in those who are preparing to teach because we are unwilling or unable to extend to them the support they need to succeed as they begin their careers. Schools and universities can collaboratively launch beginning teacher programs which will curtail the exodus of new teachers from the profession and strengthen teaching. *Designing Programs for New Teachers: The California Experience* captures the experience and knowledge of the many fine California teachers and university faculty who are working together to build beginning teacher support programs.

Foreword

Bill Honig
Superintendent
of Public Instruction
State of California

T HE quality of classroom teachers in California has never been more important than it is today. Assuming that pupil teacher ratios remain constant, the Policy Analysis for California Education (PACE) group forecast that California will need 327,500 new elementary teachers through 1994-95. Beginning in 1990-91, secondary pupil enrollments will also begin to increase, with corollary additional demands for single-subject credential holders (PACE, 1989). Where will these teachers come from? How well will they be qualified to teach the diverse California student population? What, if anything, can we do to ensure that those who are most qualified choose to stay in teaching?

California must take a comprehensive approach to addressing these issues. The various educational segments (Elementary-secondary education, California State University, University of California, Association of Independent Colleges and Universities, California Community Colleges, and others) are currently working together on a number of cooperative initiatives to address these issues. These include strategies to (1) recruit able individuals into the teaching profession; (2) provide them with the best possible preparation; (3) give new teachers ample support during their early, difficult years in the classroom; (4) establish rigorous standards for their full recognition as educational professionals; and (5) facilitate their commitment to life-long professional development.

This *Guidebook* is an important contribution to these efforts, particularly as they pertain to the support of new teachers. The articles describe various conceptions and alternative approaches to new teacher support and assessment and the multiple roles that various organizations can take to this process. The insights offered in these are particularly critical given our current shortage of teachers, the changing student population in the state, and the climate of readiness for educational reform.

Although the book does not address the issue of recruiting minorities into teaching, all of us will need to work toward a better match between the students in California classrooms and the heterogeneity in the teaching population. We need more teachers from diverse backgrounds to serve as role models for our students. In 1989-90, the racial and ethnic composition of the nation's K-12 pupil enrollment is diametrically opposed to school, college and university enrollments. At a time when more than 50 percent of K-12 students in California are racially, ethnically, and linguistically diverse, the typical classroom teacher continues to be a forty-year-old, Anglo, non-Hispanic female. Forecasts suggest that these trends will continue unless concerted efforts are made to increase the successful participation of all students in elementary, secondary, and postsecondary education. As Bud Hodgkinson has put it, "By around the year 2000, America will be a nation in which one of every *three* of us will be non-white. Minorities will cover a broader socioeconomic range than ever before, which makes simplistic treatment of their needs not useful," (Institute for Educational Leadership, 1985).

The need to recruit and support new teachers from various backgrounds is made more complex by the climate of educational reform currently pervading discussions of teaching. Historically, changes in the supply and demand of teachers in California, as elsewhere, have been managed by loosening or tightening the requirements for the teaching credential. What makes responding to the current shortfall of teachers so difficult is that we are simultaneously exploring ways to upgrade the standards for entry and performance during the early years in teaching while recruiting more individuals from diverse, dissimilar backgrounds into the occupation.

I believe we can do it. As evidenced by pilot programs in communities as diverse as San Diego, Oakland, Chico, Hayward, Fresno and Santa Cruz, young and not-so-young people are choosing careers in teaching. When provided with organizational support and staff development that recognizes their novice status, new teachers are signing up to stay in the occupation, even in hard-to-staff schools and districts. Nevertheless, new teacher support is only as good as the context in which it is embedded. In that sense, it is just one element in the larger strategy to strengthen the educational workforce through comprehensive preparation and assessment of prospective teachers, the provision of support during induction, competitive compensation packages, and working conditions which reflect responsible decision making in a climate of professional accountability.

Acknowledgements

WE wish to extend a very special expression of gratitude to Judy Shulman, Director of the Support for Beginning Teachers Program and the Institute for Case Development at Far West Laboratory. Judy has been involved in every aspect of this project. She shared her expertise and insights in the entire planning and editing process and enthusiastically contributed to the development of this book. She has been a superb collaborator and colleague, and this work would not have been possible without her having served with distinction in these roles.

We would also like to gratefully acknowledge Joan McRobbie, Writer and Editor, and Fredrika Baer, Administrative Assistant, both from Far West Laboratory, who were responsible for the final editing and design of this publication, and Patricia Christen for design suggestions.

We wish to express our sincere thanks to Susie Kidder, Coordinator for Support Services for the San Diego State University Teacher Education Reform Projects. Her organizational skills, dedication, gentle suggestions and warm heart have assisted us throughout the project and were especially invaluable during the preparation of the manuscript.

In addition to San Diego State University, this project was supported by the California State Department of Education, the Office of the Chancellor of the California State University, and Far West Laboratory for Educational Research and Development. We are especially appreciative of the assistance given to us by Laura Wagner of the State Department and Jan Mendelsohn of the Chancellor's Office.

We are also indebted to many other individuals whose assistance has made this project possible. In planning the San Diego Invitational Workshop, upon which most of this book is based, we consulted with colleagues throughout California by telephone and in small group meetings. Their advice was incorporated into the conference agenda and materials. Often these generous colleagues served as group facilitators, and some became contributors to this work.

Lastly, we want to thank the new teachers with whom we have worked. They have welcomed our assistance and provided critical comments for the improvement of our new teacher programs. Most of all, their appreciation of our efforts and their development as young professionals made us feel that what we were attempting to do was of increasing effectiveness and importance. This led us to want to capture the knowledge that we and other educators in California were acquiring in order to improve our programs for new teachers and hopefully be of use to others.

Introduction

Ann I. Morey*
San Diego State University

THIS book is intended to assist the many talented women and men who have chosen education as a career and whose work with the nation's children will touch the future in significant ways. As these new teachers enter their classrooms they face unprecedented challenges related to changes in societal context, increasing ethnic diversity, and the condition of public education. As a group, they will struggle with the transition from college student to classroom teacher; they will encounter situations where they question whether they have the necessary knowledge or problem-solving skills to respond effectively. Many will leave teaching within five years. Programs to assist these new teachers are being organized, implemented, and evaluated across the country. As a result, the knowledge base is expanding.

*The author wishes to acknowledge the contributions made by Diane Murphy, Gail Senter, and John Mergendoller to the literature review of this chapter.

In this publication we seek to capture the knowledge of California educational leaders who are involved in programs of support for new teachers. Our intent is to provide guidance for ourselves and others in the planning and implementation of programs for new teachers. Decidedly pragmatic, this book is focused on improving the quality and retention of teachers.

We also hope to provide a perspective for California policy-makers and their staffs as they frame legislation to support programs for all of California's new teachers. Certainly, this legislation will be in the context of the revenues of the state and influenced by various state-level constituent groups. It costs about $35,000 to prepare a new teacher, and the loss of this teacher within the first few years of teaching is indeed expensive to California. It is our view that we can provide effective support for new teachers that will greatly increase their retention. However, the impact of such support will be reduced if the legislation is more expedient than informed.

THE GROWTH OF NEW TEACHER ASSISTANCE PROGRAMS

Although induction programs in education began over 20 years ago, it was not until the 1980s that such programs commanded nationwide interest. In 1988, Far West Laboratory identified nineteen states and the District of Columbia where assistance programs for new teachers were being piloted or newly implemented. Further, the literature on new teacher programs has grown dramatically, reflecting a new interest and research direction.

Two major factors that have influenced this focus of attention are concern for the quality of public education and the impending teacher shortage. Each is discussed below.

Concern for quality. In recent years we have seen a flurry of national and state reports voicing dissatisfaction with the quality of public education and putting forth recommendations for its improvement (e.g., *A Nation at Risk*, National Commission on Excellence, 1983; *A Nation Prepared*, Carnegie Commission, 1986; *Tomorrow's Teachers*, Holmes Group, 1986; *Who Will Teach Our Children*? California Commission on the Teaching Profession, 1985). While the content and structure of teacher preparation programs vary among institutions and across states, key

issues have been identified and debated, and reform is well underway in many places. In California, for example, fragmentation of the teacher preparation program is an important issue. Reform efforts in this state have centered on building an integrated, coherent, and extended teacher education program and on the development of collaborative arrangements between university discipline faculty, teacher educators, and public school personnel.

In 1983, the Office of the Chancellor of the California State University issued a report on *Excellence in Professional Education* (Morey). This report spoke to the issue of fragmentation. It also reflected the judgment of many California teacher educators and public school personnel that one-year teacher credential programs inadequately prepared novices for the complexity of teaching, and an induction period of actual school teaching experience and structured support was needed. This view, shared by many across the nation, is heightened by the tremendous growth in knowledge about teaching and learning.

Education is the only profession in which the novice's responsibilities are the same or more difficult than those of veteran professionals (Borko, 1986; Darling-Hammond, 1985; Hall, 1982; Huling-Austin, 1987; Lanier with Little, 1986; Odell, 1987). Medicine, engineering, and architecture require a lengthy training period with gradual increases in assumption of responsibilities (Wise & Darling-Hammond, 1987). These and other professions have defined and refined induction and socialization programs. New architects, engineers, and psychologists, for example, must work under the direction of an established professional for a predetermined length of time before licensure. Future physicians have extended intern and residency experiences, and nurses spend two to four years under the guidance of a senior nurse. Education is still exploring and identifying the needs of novice teachers, the mechanics and governance of induction programs, and the effects of such programs.

Research has documented the critical nature of the first year of teaching (Borko, 1986; McDonald, 1980; Nemser, 1983). The new teacher's developmental growth, attitudes, feelings, style of teaching, expectations and decision to remain in teaching are all influenced by the first year experience. The individual is in transition from the familiar and comfortable roles of student and learner to teacher and, for many, to adult. Working in the real world of the classroom can result in a re-evaluation of expectations, changes in teaching behavior and belief systems, and in disillusionment (Blase, 1985; Hoy, 1968; Lortie, 1975; McMurray, Hardy & Posluns, 1987; Veenman, 1984).

Many studies have delineated the problems faced by new teachers. In an analysis of 83 studies on the perceived problems of beginning teachers, Veenman (1984) determined that the ten problems most frequently encountered in the first year of teaching are in rank order: classroom discipline, motivating students, dealing with individual differences, assessing students' work, relations with parents, organization of class work, insufficient materials and supplies, dealing with problems of individual students, heavy teaching load resulting in insufficient preparation time, and relations with colleagues. Commonality exists between problems encountered by beginning elementary and secondary teachers. Interestingly, classroom discipline is the most serious and frequent problem reported at every level. Further, some studies relate the problems encountered by beginning teachers to individual traits such as gender, age, attitude, and academic ability (e.g., Stone, 1964; Myers, Kennedy & Cruickshank, 1979; Adams & Martray, 1980). Other studies have sought to classify problems by focusing on teacher development and have identified clusters of concerns at various stages (e.g., Fuller & Bown, 1975; Clement, 1985; Adams, Hutchinson & Martray, 1980; Murphy, 1988). The underlying reason for delineating the problems of new teachers is the assumption that successful efforts which address the problems will improve the quality of teaching.

In recent years, many research and evaluation studies have been done on programs to assist new teachers. These studies vary in scope, purpose, and methodology. Huling-Austin (1988) did a synthesis of seventeen data-based research studies on induction programs and practices that had been reported since 1977. As an organizing framework for the synthesis, she identified five goals of new teacher programs and found research data to support the view that induction programs can be successful in achieving these goals. The five goals were:

1. To improve teaching performance;

2. To increase the retention of promising beginning teachers during the induction years;

3. To promote the personal and professional well-being of beginning teachers;

4. To satisfy mandated requirements related to induction and certification;

5. To transmit the culture of the system to beginning teachers.

In addition, Huling-Austin (1988) reported that the studies collectively also documented (1) the need for flexibility in induction programs, (2) the important role of the support teacher, (3) the importance of placement in beginning teacher success, and (4) the need to educate the profession (as well as the public) about teacher induction.

Huling-Austin (1986) believes that it is also important to state what induction programs cannot accomplish. She contends that induction programs cannot reasonably be expected to overcome major problems associated with school context such as misplacements in which a teacher is given: 1) misassignments—placements that do not match the teacher's discipline; 2) classrooms that are overcrowded; 3) too many preparations; and 4) placements where even veteran teachers have difficulty. Likewise, induction programs cannot turn all at risk novice teachers into professionals, nor effectively screen out weak teachers without evaluation provisions in place. Finally, although effective induction programs can impact the retention of qualified teachers during their initial years, Huling-Austin suggests that to significantly improve teacher retention long-term, we need changes in the educational system at large.

The impending teacher shortage. The goal of improving teacher quality probably would not, by itself, have spurred the current level of beginning teacher program activity. It took projections of a teacher shortage to focus state and national level attention on the supply and retention of new teachers.

It is estimated that by the year 2000, the nation will need to replace half of its 2.2 million teachers due to retirement and attrition. Yet, the supply-side picture is dismal. Only 6.2 percent of entering college students in 1988 were interested in teaching as a career; over twenty percent showed an interest two decades ago (see Schlechty & Vance, 1983; Huling-Austin, 1986). Moreover, an estimated fifty percent of all new teachers leave after five to seven years of classroom teaching, and eighty percent are gone after ten years. This attrition of teachers from education represents a tremendous loss of public investment in teacher preparation. Some do return. But even when sophisticated methods are used to estimate and incorporate return rates of teachers, the national need for teachers remains very significant.

California will need between 16,000 and 20,000 new teachers each year for the next decade. With an estimated 26,000 students enrolled in basic teacher credential programs in California, the training costs are in the hundreds of millions of dollars annually. Yet, like elsewhere, California estimates that up to half of these beginning teachers will leave teaching within five years. The high rate of attrition compounds the recruitment problems of school districts, and increases the overall costs of preparing a sufficient supply of teachers for California schools.

The reasons why teachers leave the classroom have been well documented. Conditions of work are frequently cited, including salary level, lack of career ladders, non-teaching assignments, class size and lack of adequate resources. Many teachers also leave because of frustration, isolation, unmet expectations, and a sense of helplessness over the increasingly complex demands all teachers face.

ACCOUNTABILITY AND ASSESSMENT

The publicly supported effort to improve the quality of teachers through preservice and inservice education has resulted in increased need and pressure for measuring teacher performance. Assessment is seen as a means to verify professional knowledge and competence. Such verification can support efforts for higher teacher salaries as well as become a basis for licensure and credentialing. States have experimented with different procedures for testing basic skills, assessing pedagogical competence, and certifying subject-matter expertise. In fact, the vast majority of states with new teacher support programs emphasize assessment and require a summative evaluation to determine whether a new teacher should receive state certification. The function of assistance with such programs is often to help teachers meet the assessment standards. On the other hand, programs sponsored by the District of Columbia and two states aim only to provide assistance and support, and have no formal assessment component.

THE CALIFORNIA EFFORT

School districts and, to a lesser extent, universities have always given attention to neophyte teachers. During the 1980s, this attention has become more intense and formalized. Local school initiatives were bolstered by the California Mentor Teacher Program, which paid successful teachers extra money to provide inservice education to other teachers. Further, both school and university interests were assisted by support from the federal government and private foundations. For example, the Harcourt Foundation's Scholar's Program annually selects a new cohort of twenty San Diego State University students that it then supports from their senior year in college through their third year of classroom teaching. The U.S. Department of Education, through several of its programs, has funded many projects for new teachers, including those for bilingual teachers.

Public funding in California was authorized by the legislature in 1986 as an intersegmental effort of the California State University system and the State Department of Education. Five currently funded projects entail collaboration between a CSU campus and local public schools to support new teachers in inner-city schools. The expressed purposes are to increase teaching effectiveness and improve the retention rate of new teachers.

In 1988, the California legislature authorized formation of the California New Teacher Project. In addition to developing and evaluating alternative induction programs, this project is designing and studying alternative models of teacher assessment for potential revision of state credentialing requirements. Fifteen new teacher projects were funded, and the potential collaborators with schools were broadened to include teachers' associations, county school district offices, the University of California, and private colleges and universities in addition to the California State University. It is interesting to note that eighty percent of the proposals submitted in this funding competition were school district and university collaborations. In an effort to explore alternative configurations, however, the State Department of Education and the California Commission on Teacher Credentialing funded proposals which represented a diversity of partnership models.

Thus, California by 1989 had a variety of new teacher programs funded locally, by the state and by federal and private foundation sources. Networks quickly developed among the various program and project leaders, and it became clear that many of these programs were addressing similar situations and trying to implement similar innovative ideas. Some of these innovations potentially applied to other programs throughout the state. It also became apparent that program orientations and activities matured and changed over time; older projects were significantly different from newer ones. The knowledge gained from these experiences would be transitory unless an effort was made to document the learnings and experience.

In order to capture and articulate the experiential wisdom begin gained throughout the state, the College of Education at San Diego State University organized a conference for educational leaders committed to assisting new teachers. The State Department of Education, Far West Laboratory, and the California State University system were co-sponsors.

The state-wide conference, held in March 1989, attracted eighty participants who were actively engaged in beginning teacher programs. Topics explored included frameworks, obstacles, and practical solutions for implementation, collaboration, and institutionalization of beginning teacher programs. Only a few sessions featured presentations made by experts. The vast majority were structured to gather information—individually and collectively—from the participants. Each workshop session began with participants writing responses to questions posed by the conference organizers. Next came small group discussions which were recorded and later transcribed. These materials were used by the authors of this book to capture our growing practical knowledge about programs to assist new teachers. A second workshop, co-sponsored by the California State University at Hayward and Oakland Unified School District, and Far West Laboratory focused on Bay Area proposed and current efforts to assist beginning teachers.

Knowledge gained at the San Diego conference—and to some extent the Hayward conference—are incorporated into this book. Chapter authors, each involved in the structuring of the San Diego conference, were selected for their expertise.

AN OVERVIEW OF THE BOOK

Laura Wagner (Chapter 1) provides a context for understanding state-supported programs to assist new teachers in California. One of the important factors that shapes this context is the recognized need to address the fragmentation in teacher preparation that is a result of California credentialing law. Regardless of intent, this law has resulted in the separation of subject-matter preparation from professional preservice education and from inservice education. Another critical factor is the complexity and heterogeneity of the California education and policy systems; for California, reform efforts are likely to be products of coalitions, since multiple policy and programmatic approaches are necessary to accommodate the varying political, economic, demographic, and educational conditions in the state.

Mary Gendernalik Cooper (Chapter 2) offers an astute examination of conceptual frameworks which undergird programs to assist new teachers. This examination serves the practical purpose of deepening the reader's comprehension of the operational models and approaches discussed in subsequent chapters. Cooper describes four frameworks and analyzes each framework for its efficacy in providing immediate as well as long-term assistance to beginning teachers. She maintains that without this connection to a conceptual framework, programs are less coherent and therefore less effective.

In Chapter 3, Diane S. Murphy, Katherine Merseth, and Ann I. Morey describe the content and strategies for assisting new teachers. The information presented reflects the shared knowledge and experience of beginning teacher project leaders who attended the California invitational workshops. The chapter provides useful examples of content and assistance for starting the school year as well as for improving instructional performance throughout the year. It also includes suggested adaptations of assistance necessary for large geographic regions, ethnically diverse school settings, and year-round education.

Judith H. Shulman and Victoria L. Bernhardt explain the role of experienced educators in assisting new teachers. They describe the wide-ranging services provided by public school teachers and administrators as well as district staff and university faculty to assist new teachers. The selection of these "assistors" and their appropriate matching with new teachers are critical elements in the success of the program. The authors conclude the chapter with a set of recommendations to consider when planning a new teacher support program.

In Chapter 5, Bernhardt and Shulman turn their attention specifically to the role of universities in new teacher programs. They note that universities and school districts increasingly recognize the need for integrated, continuous and relevant instruction from the college years through the professional development years. Thus, teacher preparation institutions working with public school practitioners are devising extended curricula for professional teaching. Each partner can make unique as well as similar contributions to the development of new teachers.

Louise Bay Waters, Carolyn Cates, and Cynthia Harris (Chapter 6) address two questions: What personnel, programs, organizations, and other resources are necessary to achieve project outcomes? How can support be generated for the beginning teacher project? They describe district offices' contributions of staff development, mentor programs, and personnel, as well as the contributions of teachers' associations, universities, and county offices of education.

Seven new teacher projects are highlighted in Chapter 7. They were chosen to represent the diversity of organizational structures, providers, content, strategies for assistance, and conceptual frameworks that typify the California effort. The first two projects described (Oakland-CSU Hayward, and San Diego) are in their fourth year and represent university-school district relationships that are dynamic and focused on continually improving support for new teachers. The Oakland-Hayward description gives a four-year retrospective that is extremely useful because it documents problems faced by many projects at the initial stages of implementation and provides information about the successive steps taken to find optimum solutions. In contrast, the San Diego description focuses more on the conceptual framework for the project and the translation of this framework into actual project activities.

The next four projects described are in their second year of operation. The Poway program is a collaboration between a school district and a teachers' union. Full-time experienced teachers working under the guidance of a Peer Review Board provide individual on-site assistance to new teachers and also conduct assessments of teaching performance. The CSU Chico program, which serves a huge geographic area involving numerous school districts, uses interactive instructional television to provide instructional seminars and to reinforce the relationships established among advisors, beginning teachers, and university personnel. The Santa Clara project is an example of a school district-designed and implemented program emphasizing time and classroom management. Mentor teachers and on-site support teachers assist new teachers through one-on-one consultations and class visits, seminars, and workshops. The Santa Cruz program is a consortium effort among county offices of education, seven school districts, and a university. Recognizing that new teachers enter the profession at different developmental stages and with individual needs, each new teacher develops and occasionally updates an individualized plan and works with an exemplary teacher. Lastly, the El Cajon/San Diego project, a collaborative project between a school district and a university, is a three-phase induction model based on a developmental stage concept with assistance in the last phase drawing upon the resources of a professional development school.

In Chapter 8, Douglas E. Mitchell and David Hough provide a thought-provoking policy framework for new teacher support. They begin by defining and examining five possible labor market strategies for improving the number and quality of California teachers. In doing so, they pose criteria for determining whether induction programs are the most effective and efficient market strategy, and they offer an analysis of whether conditions warrant investment in new teacher programs.

If decision-makers choose to concentrate resources in induction programs as a labor market strategy, then what orientations or patterns of support should shape the content of the programs? Mitchell and Hough offer a typology for categorizing programs that is based on whether skills and knowledge or collegial relationships command more attention, and whether the primary focus is directed locally at the school site or more generally to the profession *in toto*. The typology provides a useful tool for analyzing the relative emphases of different components within an actual program. Lastly, the authors identify seven key players in induction programs and note that it is difficult to know how to distribute the appropriate mixture of responsibility and authority.

Perhaps Wagner's observation about the complexity of California and the need for a variety of collaborative models is helpful here.

Gary D. Estes, Kendyll Stansbury, and Claudia Long (Chapter 9) focus attention on the important matter of assessing teacher knowledge, skills, and performance. Like other states, California is seeking to evaluate individual teachers through the use of particular instruments that purport to assess teacher competence. Based on their work, the authors conclude that assessments which more authentically represent the knowledge and skills required for teaching can help shape assistance to beginning teachers, clarify the domains that are critical for teachers, and increase public confidence in the quality of the teaching force.

This book is not meant as a prescriptive manual, but rather as a useful tool for those individuals and groups who are planning and implementing programs to assist new teachers. We hope to provide some encouragement, stimulate reflection and improve our collective efforts to support beginning teachers and ultimately to enhance the education of the nation's children. We also hope to highlight policy and assessment issues and to raise people's consciousness about the complexity of teaching. We want to inform the development of guidelines and legislation that provide structure, and at the same time foster flexibility so that local entities can maximize their efforts.

REFERENCES

Adams, R., & Martray, C. (1980). *Correlates of teacher perceived problems*. Paper presented at the 9th annual conference of the Mid-South Educational Research Association, New Orleans. (ERIC Document No. ED 195 567).

Adams, R., Hutchinson, S., & Martray, C. (1980). *A developmental study of teacher concerns across time*. Paper presented at the annual meeting of the American Research Association, Boston.

Blase, J.J. (1985). The socialization of teachers: An ethnographic study of factors contributing to the rationalization of the teacher's instructional perspective. *Urban Education, 20*(3), 235-256.

Borko, H. (1986). Clinical teacher education: The induction years. In J. Hoffman & S. Edwards (Eds.), *Reality and reform in clinical teacher education*, NY: Random House.

Fuller, F., & Bown, O. (1975). On becoming a teacher. In K. Ryan (Ed.), *Teacher Education*. The 74th National Society for the Study of Education Yearbook. Chicago: University of Chicago Press.

California Commission on the Teaching Profession. (1985). *Who will teach our children? A strategy for improving California schools*.

California State University. (1983). *Excellence in professional education, a report of the advisory committee to study programs in education*, Ann I. Morey, Chair. Long Beach, CA: California State University.

Carnegie Forum on Education and the Economy Task Force on Teaching as a Profession. (1986). *A nation prepared: teachers for the 21st century*. New York: Carnegie Corporation.

Clement, B. (1985). *Beginning teachers' use of classroom management*. Research and Development Center for Teacher Education, Texas University. (ERIC Document No. ED 263 110)

Darling-Hammond, L. (1985). Valuing teachers: The making of a profession. *Teachers College Record, 87*(2), 205-218.

Hall, G.E. (1982). Induction: The missing link. *Journal of Teacher Education, 33*(3), 53-55.

Holmes Group, Inc. (1986). *Tomorrow's teachers: A report of The Holmes Group*. East Lansing, MI: The Holmes Group.

Hoy, W. (1968). The influence of experience on the beginning teacher. *Journal of Educational Research, 66*, 89-93.

Huling-Austin, L. (1986). What can and cannot reasonably be expected from teacher induction programs. *Journal of Teacher Education*, 37(1), 2-5.

Huling-Austin, L. (1987). Teacher induction. In D.M. Brooks (Ed.), *Teacher induction—A new begin-*

ning (pp. 3-24). Reston, VA: Association of Teacher Educators.

Huling-Austin, L. (1988). *A synthesis of research on teacher induction programs and practices.* Paper presented at the annual meeting of the American Educational Research Association, New Orleans, LA.

Lanier, J.E., with Little, J.W. (1986). Research on teacher education. In M.C. Wittrock (Ed.), *Handbook of research on teaching* (pp. 527-569). NY: Macmillan.

Lortie, D.C. (1975). *School teacher: A sociological study.* Chicago: University of Chicago Press.

McDonald, F. (1980). *The problems of beginning teachers: A crisis in training. Study of induction programs for beginning teachers* (Vol. 1). Princeton, NY: Educational Testing Service.

McMurray, J., Hardy, M., & Posluns, R. (1987). *Successful life experiences, teaching styles and stress in beginning teachers.* Paper presented at the American Educational Research Association, Boston.

Murphy, D.S. (1988). The impact of socialization mechanisms on the problem-solving approaches of novice teachers. (Doctoral Dissertation: The Claremont Graduate School/San Diego State University Joint Doctoral Program in Education).

Myers, B., Kennedy, J., & Cruickshank, D. (1979). Relationship of teacher personality variables to teacher perceived problems. *Journal of Teacher Education*, 30(6), 33-40.

National Commission on Excellence in Education. (1983). *A nation at risk: The imperative for educational reform.* Washington, DC: GPO.

Nemser, S.F. (1983). Learning to teach. In L.S. Shulman & G. Sykes (Eds.), *Handbook of teaching and policy* (pp. 150-169). NY: Longman.

Odell, S. (1987). Teacher induction: Rationale and issues. In D.M. Brooks (Ed.), *Teacher induction— A new beginning* (pp. 69-80). Reston, VA: Association of Teacher Educators.

Schlechty, P.C., & Vance, V.S. (1983). Recruitment, selection and retention: The shape of the teaching force. *The Elementary School Journal, 83*(4), 469-487.

Stone, E. (1964). Personal and professional problems recognized by beginning, junior and senior high school teachers and the relation to the number of their problems to personal characteristics, professional preparation, teacher assignment and career plans. *Dissertation Abstracts International, 25*, 2808.

Veenman, S. (1984). Perceived problems of beginning teachers. *Review of Educational Research, 54*, (2), 143-178.

Wise, A., Darling-Hammond, L., Berry, B., & Klein, S.P. (1987). *Licensing teachers: Design for a teacher profession.* Santa Monica, CA: The Rand Corporation.

CHAPTER 1

A Context for Analyzing State Supported New Teacher Reform Efforts in California

Laura A. Wagner*

State Department of Education

ACTIVITIES to support new teachers in California are part of a larger mission to prepare, license, and encourage staff development for California's K-12 educators in a comprehensive fashion. The purpose of this chapter is to provide a state policy framework for analyzing these new teacher issues. The central ideas to be addressed include the central purpose of the new teacher reforms in California, the policy system in which reforms are positioned, some examples of preservice preparation and new teacher support programs, and lessons from the implementation literature to give direction to new teacher reform activities.

* The views expressed in this article are the opinion of the author and are not official positions of the California State Department of Education.

THE PURPOSE OF TEACHER EDUCATION REFORMS

In recent decades, teacher induction in California has been fragmented. Undergraduate work toward the baccalaureate has been separated from teacher preparation, which has itself been separated from organized learning activities for teachers once they are working in their own classrooms. Teacher credentialing has attended primarily to candidate literacy and standards for teacher preparation programs with fairly modest attention to assurances that individuals demonstrate curricular instructional competence with diverse student groups. California is currently investigating the need to change its teacher credentialing requirement. There are currently two levels of teacher credentials in California: a preliminary credential and a clear credential. To receive a preliminary credential in California, candidates must be recommended by a California teacher preparation institution with a program approved by the Commission on Teacher Credentialing. To receive this recommendation candidates must:

- complete a baccalaureate or higher degree from a regionally accredited college or university

- complete a single subject or multiple subject professional teacher preparation program, including student teaching, with a minimum grade of B

- pass the California Basic Educational Skills Test (CBEST), intended to assess basic adult literacy in reading, writing and mathematics

- complete a course (two semester units or three quarter units) in the provisions and principles of the United States Constitution or pass an examination on the Constitution

- complete a course in the methods of teaching reading or pass the National Teacher Examination entitled "Introduction to the Teaching of Reading," and

- verify subject-matter competency by:

  - obtaining a subject-matter waiver statement from the authorized person in the education department of a California college or university with a Commission-approved waiver program verifying completion of a subject-specific program (liberal studies or diversified subjects concentration for multiple subject, or content-specific concentration for single subject), or

  - by achieving a passing score on the appropriate subject-matter area examination given by the National Teacher Examinations (content-specific for single subject, or general knowledge core battery for multiple subject).

The preliminary credential is issued for a maximum of five years.

To receive a professional clear credential an applicant must:

- complete a fifth year of study after the bachelor's degree

- complete a unit requirement in health education, including, but not limited to, information about nutrition, the physiological and sociological effects of abuse of alcohol, narcotics, and drugs, and the use of tobacco

- complete a requirement in the needs for and methods of providing educational opportunities to individuals with exceptional needs (mainstreaming), and

- satisfactorily complete a computer education course which includes general and specialized skills in the use of computers in educational settings.

An applicant must have a grade point average of C or that required by the approved institution, whichever is higher, in all coursework offered toward fulfillment of credential requirements. *

There are a variety of alternative routes into teaching and individuals with specific questions about teacher credential qualifications should contact a credential counselor with the Commission on Teacher Credentialing, Sacramento, California

Once in the workforce, teachers tend to pursue coursework in self-selected areas which may or may not be related to developing knowledge and skill related to the subjects they teach. At the same time, their increased knowledge and skill is only weakly related to advancement in the profession, either as a master or mentor teacher or in another leadership role. Thus, a fundamental purpose of the teaching improvement effort is to create a more comprehensive system of new teacher preparation, credentialing, induction support, ongoing professional development and diverse career growth opportunities, where the content of these activities is better articulated.

THE POLICY SYSTEM FOR INITIATING NEW TEACHER REFORM EFFORTS

Given the broad array of issues underlying reform in teacher preparation, credentialing, and induction, the challenge for state and local school educators and university professors is to experiment with manageable pieces of the reforms and provide opportunity for multiple alternative approaches to develop locally, prior to making recommendations for system-wide implementation. However, an underlying assumption here is that ultimately, any statewide system needs to have clear goals, establish rigorous standards for new teacher preparation and accountability, and provide broad flexibility for implementation in varying local contexts. Further, a statewide system needs to take into account the complexity of the California policy system. Susan Fuhrman (1989), with the Eagleton Institute of Policy Studies at Rutgers University, provides an interesting viewpoint on the California policy system:

> State politics and culture are strong influences on the course of reform. The size and complexity of California, the heterogeneity of teacher-student populations, massive electorate and weak political party system boost the importance of any state-wide elected officials. Further, to mandate anything in California is almost prohibitively expensive because of the size of the system and the high portion of funding that comes from the state in the post-Proposition 13 era. The state is required to fully fund any mandates. Hence California relies heavily on inducements to local districts to implement reform (pp. 61-75).

The implications of the complexity and heterogeneity of the California system on reform efforts are several. First, reform initiatives are likely to be the product of coalitions, rather than individuals; second, limited resources tend to be allocated to those ready to experiment with change rather than to everyone on a formula basis; and third, there is a general expectation that multiple policy and programmatic approaches will be necessary to accommodate the varying political, economic, demographic and educational conditions in the state. Several examples follow which illustrate these policy approaches. In each case, the initiative is collaborative, limited to those evidencing readiness for change, and tied to a larger effort of informing future state policy.

EXAMPLES OF NEW TEACHER PREPARATION AND SUPPORT PROGRAMS

The Comprehensive Teacher Education Institutes

The purpose of the Teacher Education Institutes, jointly funded in 1988-1989 by the California State University (CSU) and the State Department of Education at $690,000, is to reform teacher preparation programs over a four-year period through three-way partnerships. Funding is provided for school districts, university subject-matter departments, and schools of education to cooperatively redesign and strengthen teacher preparation programs to make them more field based and responsive to the learning needs of California's prospective new teachers. The goal is that these collaborative programs will prepare highly qualified teachers who are able to work effectively with students from diverse backgrounds.

Six CSU campuses and one University of California (UC) site are currently implementing Teacher Education Institutes. Two projects, one at San Diego State University and a second at California Polytechnic State University, San Luis Obispo, are in their fourth implementation year. Five new projects at the CSU campuses at San Francisco, Chico, Fresno, Northridge, and at University of California, Riverside, are just beginning the implementation process for 1989-90. Although each of the seven projects is expected to vary in program design and implementation, the following state goals shape implementation of the locally developed plans:

- Establishment of a collaborative decision-making process for teacher preparation

- Provision of an integrated curricular and instructional program which helps candidates develop expertise in effective teaching of diverse student populations

- Articulation of undergraduate, graduate, and student teaching components

- Assessment of teacher candidate knowledge and skills

- Innovative approaches to postsecondary instructional delivery

- Recruitment of underrepresented groups into teaching, and

- Articulation between preservice preparation and inservice support.

Each Teacher Education Institute is intended to be a catalyst for educational change in teacher preparation programs. Funds serve as a mechanism for self-study, restructuring, and experimentation with alternative techniques of teacher preparation. In the process, the institutional partners review and assess the current teacher preparation programs, select mutually agreed-upon Institute goals; design and implement a plan to achieve those goals, and develop a plan for institutionalizing the most effective practices once state funding ceases at the end of the fourth year.

The San Luis Obispo and San Diego Institutes have created collaborative work groups which generate, shape, promote, and implement innovative teacher education proposals. At both sites, the Institute has revamped the formal advisory structure that provides input into the key policy making committees that oversee the teacher preparation process. However, because the contexts differ, the focus of each project differs.

The Teacher Education Institute at San Diego State University has focused a substantial part of its attention on the development of an experimental on-site teacher preparation program at Crawford High School as well as on the development of a collaborative decision-making process. Some of the key features of the program are:

- An ongoing and systematic decision-making process that includes the academic depart-

ments, the College of Education, and local school district personnel as partners in the development and implementation of the teacher preparation program,

- Collaborative instructional arrangements among College of Education faculty, academic department faculty, and public school teachers, placing emphasis on the integration of subject matter content and pedagogy,

- Coordinated advising and supervision of candidates by master teachers, education faculty, and academic department faculty

- A significant increase in the number of school-based experiences in courses required for the prospective teacher, and

- A public school-site based program providing a classroom for university instruction and provision of a physical space where student teachers can give each other peer support and meet with campus and school-site faculty.

By contrast, the Institute at San Luis Obispo serves as a catalyst for a number of initiatives and programs. Some of these include:

- Appointment of public school teachers as adjunct professors who serve in the teacher education program

- Expansion of the master teacher training program, including development of clinical instructors to serve as resources for cooperating teachers, and

- Expanded team teaching experiences to give prospective teachers opportunities for early field experiences.

The Comprehensive Teacher Education Institute Projects at San Francisco State University; CSU Northridge; CSU Chico; CSU Fresno; and the University of California at Riverside are still in their infancy, though each has initiated some activity. The Fresno Institute is planning to orient university faculty to the contents of K-12 instruction. San Francisco State has a multi-faceted approach in which five task forces are developing integrated training and assessment activities for new teachers in curriculum and instruction for heterogeneous student groups. UC Riverside is planning to undertake a Professional Development School.

Regardless of approach, the Teacher Education Institute effectiveness brings a commitment from the multiple participants, including local school district personnel, teacher education faculty, and faculty in university arts and sciences programs. In addition to collaboration, several other policy issues are emerging as important for program implementation, as reported in the external evaluation of the pilot programs.

- School districts and universities differ dramatically in organization and culture, and special efforts need to be made by each system to facilitate communication and resource allocation procedures.

- Because each Institute grant is relatively small and of limited duration, Institute goals need to be focused and concrete so there is a reasonable opportunity for reform efforts to be implemented and institutionalized.

- The Teacher Education Institute is a "change strategy" rather than a specified set of activities for high fidelity implementation. In other words, the initiative must co-exist with other institutional structures, and cannot initiate reforms unless they complement local readiness for change.

The Inner City New Teacher Retention Project

Legislatively authorized as an intersegmental effort of the CSU system in collaboration with the State Department of Education, the purpose of the New Teacher Retention Project is to support new teachers in inner city schools in order to increase their teaching effectiveness and improve their retention rates.

Five CSU campuses (Hayward, San Diego, San Francisco, Northridge, and Dominguez Hills) are working with new teachers in four inner city school districts. Two projects, one in San Diego and a second in Oakland, are in their fourth implementation year. Two new projects, one in San Francisco and one in the greater Los Angeles area, are completing their first year of implementation. Combined, the projects are providing service to approximately 400 new teachers. Because the contexts differ, each of the projects is providing teachers with somewhat different services. Nevertheless, in each project, teachers:

- Work with experienced teacher partners

- Receive instructional support from peer teachers and university faculty

- Are released from classroom responsibilities to observe and plan instruction, and

- Receive scholarships for university graduate level study and a stipend for instructional materials.

In both the San Diego and the Oakland/Hayward projects, new teacher support services are differentiated to reflect new teacher needs and the date when new teachers are hired. (Approximately half of the new teachers are not hired until after the onset of the school year.) Those receiving the more intense services have more direct contact with mentor teachers, university faculty, and district staff developers.

Two additional projects, in San Francisco and Los Angeles, are in their initial implementation year. Each site received about $100,000 for implementation activities, which include appointment of school site teams for the development of new teachers' cooperative learning skills, on-site observation and assistance of new teachers by university faculty, release time for new teachers to work with other teachers, seminars conducted by university faculty and district mentor teachers, and a university-staffed telephone hotline.

Evaluation data from the two original projects indicate that over 90 percent of the teachers originally served by the two programs are still teaching in urban schools with 81 percent still working in inner city, high minority schools. In 1986-87, the two projects served 50 teachers, and 80 teachers were served in 1987-88; 90 percent of all these are still teaching in urban settings. Important differences between secondary teachers participating in the project and a comparison group of new teachers emerged from the project evaluation. All participating secondary teachers received satisfactory or better ratings on the district teacher evaluation system; in contrast, 12.5 percent of the comparison new teachers were rated unsatisfactory in providing a suitable learning environment for their students.

In addition to enhanced teacher retention, the New Teacher Retention Projects have had other positive effects. New teacher participants demonstrated stronger classroom management skills, more diverse pedagogical skills and commitment to professional development than their non-project peers. The Retention Project evaluation has also provided insights into effective strategies for university faculty working with new teachers in inner city settings. For instance, seminars and assistance need to be practical while helping teachers develop self-analytic and reflective skills and the ability to adapt instruction to the needs of their diverse student populations.

The California New Teacher Project

The California New Teacher Project builds upon and extends the lessons learned from the Inner City New Teacher Retention Program. The California New Teacher Project is a legislatively authorized evaluation study, funded in 1989-90 at $4.5 million, to study alternative models of new teacher support and assessment. The overall purpose of the initiative is to recommend a strategy to the California Legislature for comprehensive induction and retention of well-prepared classroom teachers. Such a strategy will need to reflect the particular demands put on new teachers and make cost-effective use of resources in a candidate-based credentialing assessment system supported by staff development opportunities.

The Commission on Teacher Credentialing and the State Department of Education share the administrative responsibility for the program. New teacher support programs are underway in more than 100 school districts, some of which are working independently, while others are working with teachers' organizations and colleges and universities, either in small partnerships or in large consortia. In addition to providing information about staff development needs of new teachers, the California New Teacher Project is piloting a variety of complex measures of teacher performance to inform the Legislature about the need for more performance-based measures of teaching, as part of professional credentialing and staff development requirements.

More than 900 teachers are currently participating in the local pilot projects. Each new teacher participant is engaged in a program of professional development with the assistance of experienced colleagues. Preliminary data from the initial program evaluation indicate that new teachers are supported in two primary modes, although the support varies in intensity. These include:

- experienced teacher support, both to meet the initial "new job," or "start-up" and to help the new teacher learn or reinforce curricular, instructional, and managerial assessment skills, and

- staff development training, inservice courses or workshops provided by districts and universities on a broad range of issues.

In the assessment component of the California New Teacher Project, local project teachers and administrators are assisting the state in piloting a variety of new teacher performance assessments. In addition to materials-based paper and pencil assessments, these include structured interviews to assess the ability of a teacher to teach subject matter, and classroom observations of actual instruction. A variety of other performance assessments are in development for piloting with New Teacher Project participants in the coming year. At this point, none of these instruments is intended for ultimate adoption in a California credentialing system. Rather, the study is exploring the feasibility of these prototypes as modes of assessment, either for credentialing or to guide staff development decision-making.

The multi-year evaluation of the New Teacher Project is examining a variety of issues, including the cost effectiveness of the various support and assessment activities in:

- retaining capable new teachers,

- improving their pedagogical content knowledge and skill,

- improving their ability to teach students who are ethnically, culturally, economically, academically and linguistically diverse,

- identifying new teachers in need of assistance, and

- making careers in education more appealing to prospective teachers.

Each of these initiatives — the Comprehensive Teacher Education Institutes, the New Teacher Retention Project in Inner City Schools, and the California New Teacher Project, is examining different, but related, parts of the teacher preparation and induction process. To form an integrated system, they must also be linked to effective teacher recruitment and selection practices and to local career opportunities for classroom teachers in professional development and leadership roles.

Pilot Initiatives to Improve the Recruitment and Selection of California's Classroom Teachers

The majority of students in California's public schools are from non-European, ethnic backgrounds. By contrast, most of their teachers are white, non-Hispanic women. The percentages of teachers from the majority ethnic groups is disproportionately low, with the K-12 system employing only seven percent Hispanic and 5.8 percent Black faculty. These are disturbing statistics. Non-white teachers are important role models for non-white students. Perhaps more important, racism and racial segregation can be reduced when persons of different racial or ethnic backgrounds cooperatively interact around rewarding activities (Hawley, 1989).

To respond to these concerns, the Education Roundtable, composed of the leadership of various educational segments in California, charged a subcommittee on teaching improvement with initiating teacher recruitment efforts. Teachers, administrators, and representatives of each of the postsecondary educational segments are represented on the subcommittee. In April of 1989, the committee sponsored a workshop where 32 district and university teams developed local plans for identifying and supporting minorities who might pursue careers in teaching. In a departure from traditional conference practice, participants used the occasion to build work plans for encouraging more minorities to consider careers in teaching. Existing programs such as Project Socrates in Los Angeles and the San Jose State consortium were described. In these programs, students in middle school and high school serve as tutors for younger students and receive academic and personal counseling support for their own participation in high school, college and postgraduate preparation for teaching. As a follow-up, the CSU and the State Department of Education issued planning grants in 1989 for implementing local recruitment strategies.

Significant progress is being made. Projects like these need to be undertaken on a much larger scale if the educational community is to effectively balance the heterogeneity of the student and teacher populations.

Resources to Support More Local Career Opportunities for Classroom Teachers

Strengthening teacher preparation, credentialing, and induction support are only one part of a comprehensive system for new teacher development. Rigorous teacher evaluation practices "owned" by the practitioners themselves, as well as opportunities for experienced teachers to take local leadership roles, will be essential if our best teachers are to sustain careers in teaching.

Experienced teachers need to be rewarded by greater opportunity, more alternatives, and additional career incentives to motivate them to continue doing a good job and commit to staying in the profession. These should be encouraged within a broad framework of expanded teacher work roles. There are already a variety of site and district leadership roles which experienced teachers can pursue.

Chief among these is the California Mentor Teacher Program, which funded more than 10,500 teachers in 1988-89 to work in staff development roles. Mentor teachers do a broad array of work, including developing curriculum, helping new teachers, and participating in school site improvement efforts and conducting district staff development activities. The framework within which successful mentoring occurs is set by both the individual and the district with the mentor's activities geared toward making a long-term positive difference for individuals at the school. This framework is not always present.

For the most part, mentor teacher work is substantive. However, the differential status of the mentor role has in some cases been minimized, with mentors assigned "project" status, quasi-administrative functions, or required to put in a designated number of hours in return for the stipend. This is unfortunate, and over the next few years special efforts will be made regionally and locally to strengthen the mentor teacher's leadership role in overall school improvement efforts and in dissemination of effective teaching practices to new and veteran faculty.

There are other things that teacher leaders can do besides becoming a mentor teacher or an administrator. Some of these include:

- working as adjunct university faculty teaching prospective and novice teachers skills such as student and instructional time management, curriculum development, and how to adjust content and materials to reflect student diversity,

- developing curriculum content and materials for specific student populations,

- developing subject-specific benchmark activities and other assessments,

- site-level leadership in school improvement, the integration of categorical and core program curricula, and the formation and development of professional development activities, and

- collaborative participation in university-based action research and development.

California State Senate Bill 1882, Chapter 1362 (Morgan, 1988) has been funded to support comprehensive approaches to professional development and career opportunities in 1989-90. However, rather than initiating a separate categorical program, the legislation focuses state-funded staff development programs on school-site needs related to strengthening subject matter and instruction.

The school and its classroom teachers are identified in SB1882 as targets for the design of professional development activities which are organized chiefly around school improvement needs, rather than solely around personal interest in external workshops and courses. A second component of the legislation authorizes the establishment of resource agencies or consortia to design and provide staff development where local capacity is lacking. A third component focuses on expanding the subject matter knowledge and instructional strategies of classroom teachers through state-wide projects organized around the California Writing/Literature Project model. Each of these efforts reflects the desire to instill a more "cultural" view of professional development where classroom teachers access professional development opportunities within a school improvement context, as an alternative to participating in external short-term workshops provided by experts (Lambert, in press).

Professional development and leadership opportunities need to be coupled with better working conditions for teachers — competitive salaries, opportunities for planning, working with other teachers, and working with students in class sizes adjusted to student needs. Unless working conditions improve to the point where teachers command the respect of the adult community and feel valued in the work setting, even the best teacher preparation, induction, and staff development programs won't retain them.

The next section reviews lessons learned from the research on implementation of educational innovation; lessons which should serve as a good resource base for implementing teacher education reforms.

LESSONS FROM THE IMPLEMENTATION LITERATURE

Twenty years of research on the implementation of educational innovations gives us considerable guidance about what to expect in designing a comprehensive new teacher preparation and support strategy.

Knowledge about effective practice is critical for successful implementation at the service delivery level (McLaughlin, 1987). Practitioners need specific training in effective implementation practices, or must be shown how to adapt existing strategies for that purpose. For example, the expansion of training for mentor teachers is preparing them for, among other things, working with beginning teachers. However, we cannot always assume that individuals "have the knowledge" and only need resources to put it to use. Opportunity for staff development during the regular instructional day is an important approach to new teacher support.

The organizational location of the responsibility for implementing a change strategy or innovation makes a difference (Rossman, Corbett & Firestone, 1988). Categorical program directors, who are frequently hired "to implement" a program tend to be outside the responsible authority "lines" in implementing organizations. They have been hired to address a specific problem or issue. At the same time, the local staff person with the expertise may not be the individual with the line authority. If the issues driving the initiative and the changes brought by the program are to have staying power, they need the attention and support, if not the direct assistance, of those with line responsibility (e.g. principals, assistant superintendents, or deans). This makes it important for both individuals, the "expert" and the "line authority" to work together to change practice and develop strategies for institutionalization. That way, the program can, over time, become part of the institutional way of doing business, and resources will be more likely to be present to help make local practitioners expert in effective practices (McLaughlin, 1987).

Some resource stability is critical for successful implementation of costly innovations. One key to the likelihood of successful innovation is the degree to which participants perceive that support for an innovation will continue even when non-local resources are expended (Whitford, 1987). It is ironic that the very nature of "experimental" programs indicates a temporary resource base while getting real commitment to a program requires that those who commit the energy to it can anticipate long-term as well as short-term support. In each of the pilot programs cited above, the stronger implementation sites are that way in part because local implementors are "owning the program," finding local resources to help offset the state costs, and beginning early on to find ways to institutionalize the powerful components of their programs.

Implementation of new initiatives tends to be on the margin of organizational work, where special sub-units can be created to "handle" the problem. Witness the proliferation of school lunches, interdistrict transportation, and categorical programs for the disadvantaged (Kirst, 1984). The net effect of having programs outside the technical core, however, is fragmentation. The categorical programs "take on a life of their own," asserting the never-ending needs of their client group and failing to intersect with key related initiatives. Thus, the New Teacher Project — which is a pilot staff development program for prospective new teachers — needs to be linked organizationally with staff development for experienced teachers, and provide the kinds of support most needed by individuals in specific contexts. To be sure, categorical programs arise to provide focused attention on individuals in need of specific services, whether students or teachers; however, those who fund and implement them need to ensure that services are provided within the framework of a comprehensive approach, rather than as separate, categorical programs on the fringes of the regular system.

Implementation strategies will vary depending upon the understanding of the goal, the activities designed to reach it, the local context, and the population of individuals participating in the innovation. Implementation is the process of assembling the organizational elements or pieces needed to make the grand strategy work (Bardach, 1989). Individual program objectives and strategies differ significantly across the various teacher preparation and new teacher induction programs cited above. This is totally appropriate provided that each addresses significant objectives and is organized to reflect the needs of the population of individuals being served. For instance, the various new teacher support programs reflect the heterogeneity of California's diverse teacher and student populations. Staff development in inner cities has to be offered at times when individuals can access it. For many, during school and after-school activities are appropriate; for others, Saturdays and summers are better suited to accommodate working and personal schedules. In other settings, the relative geographic isolation among teachers, teacher trainers, and institutions of higher education means that teleconferencing and other long-distance learning strategies are most appropriate. Thus, we see instances of key staff trained as "trainers," then rotate to provide site-level teacher assistance; and programs where teachers are brought together through telecommunications to discuss common problems.

CONCLUSIONS

Several conclusions can be drawn from this. A central one is that we cannot expect a single model of new teacher preparation, support, or career opportunity to arise, any more than we can expect that one approach to instructional pedagogy will work with all students. Rather, state policies developed for broader system-wide implementation have to reflect the diverse needs of the state's student teacher and novice teacher populations.

Similarly, no one organization can provide all of the needed services. Colleges and universities have a central role in teacher preparation, but they may also play a significant role in supporting new teachers in the classroom. Similarly, local school districts are likely to be excellent laboratories for clinical training of prospective teachers. There are also some local school districts with strong capacities to provide services for new teachers without the assistance of institutions of higher education. Institutions of higher education will be the major player in providing new teacher support. But some local school districts are also able to take this role. Interestingly, research suggests that where multiple agencies are providing support, an equitable balance of service from the district and the university is critical for program success (Southwest Regional Educational Laboratory, 1989). This confirms the value of a truly collaborative relationship among agencies.

When asked to assume new roles, people need assistance and preparation. Whether new teachers, new teacher support providers, or administrators expanding group participation in decision-making, we each need the opportunity to develop new knowledge and skill in non-threatening, supported environments. Mentors, principals, and site leaders need training in their roles as supporters of new teachers. New teacher coaches and college and university support personnel need help learning how to work with new teachers in their classrooms. Administrators, teachers, and program developers may need training in more complex approaches to new teacher assessment and support. The kinds of assistance that individuals need will vary by context, role, prior knowledge and expectation, but our plans should provide opportunities and revenues for training, rather than assuming that individuals can assume new roles in human service organizations which reflect, rather than lend, the wider culture. Stated succinctly:

> At the heart of strategy is implementation; at the heart of implementation is cooperation; at the heart of cooperation is the creation and maintenance of helpful environments (Bardach, 1989).

The described initiatives are driven by a comprehensive vision of a well-prepared generation of new teachers. Cooperation and coordination of effort in supportive teaching environments will be essential if prospective and novice teachers are to enter and be rewarded by the education profession. It is never too soon to begin institutionalizing effective practice. Although some fear that collaboration and coordination with others may obscure their own agenda, such efforts often make both initiatives stronger. (A good example is the gradual incorporation of student performance data on state assessments with local data collection efforts to inform site and district decision-making about programs.) Given the anticipated complexities of 21st century society and work, the task of teachers will be enormous. Getting new teachers ready to meet the challenge is critical.

References

Bardach, E. (1989, June). Session Summary: State and Local Executive Institute. Berkeley, CA: Graduate School of Public Policy, University of California.

Fuhrman, S. (1989). State politics and education reform. *The politics of reforming school administration*. New York: Taylor and Francis.

Hawley, W. (1989). The importance of minority teachers to the racial and ethnic integration of American society. *Equity and Choice*, 5,(2).

Kirst, M. (1984). *Who controls our schools? American values in conflict*. New York: W.H. Freeman and Company.

Lambert, L. (In press). The end of staff development. *ASCD yearbook on staff development*.

McLaughlin, M. (1987). Lessons from past implementation research. *Educational Evaluation and Policy Analysis*, 9,(2).

Rossman, G., Corbett, H., & Firestone, W. (1988). *Change and effectiveness in schools*. Albany, NY: State University of New York Press.

Southwest Regional Educational Laboratory. (1989). *Year II external study of new teacher retention projects*. Los Alamitos, CA.

Whitford, B. (1987). Effects of organizational context on program implementation. In G. Noblit & W. Pink,(Eds.), *Schooling in social context*. New Jersey: Ablex Publishing.

CHAPTER 2

Conceptual Frameworks and Models of Assistance to New Teachers

Mary Gendernalik Cooper
San Diego State University

T HIS chapter describes and examines alternative conceptual frameworks which undergird efforts to assist new teachers. Such frameworks may be intentional, used to deliberately guide or shape the assistance effort. Their presence and influence can be more tacit, however; embedded in the specific activities of the assistance effort, but never clearly articulated nor employed as the guiding standard for determining the assistance activities. The conceptual frameworks represent, and therefore, reveal orientations to, beliefs about, and operational meanings of three core concepts: **teacher**, **teaching**, and **assistance**.

Approaches to assisting new teachers generally reflect one of three conceptual frameworks, each distinct from the others in terms of how it essentially defines or understands the three core concepts. Each of these conceptual frameworks reflects a distinct epistemological tradition or set of standards and beliefs upon which knowledge claims and conceptual definitions are based. A fourth, conceptually eclectic, approach to assisting new teachers also is examined. This approach is predicated on concerns teachers demonstrate rather than on qualities or characteristics which define **teacher** or **teaching**.

Each framework and the attendant meaning of the core concepts is summarized below. The discussion then proceeds to examine the relationship between conceptual frameworks and operational models of assistance. These relationships are characteristically reciprocal and dynamic; they also can be contradictory. The chapter concludes with a brief discussion of some of the forces likely to influence the shape and substance of those relationships.

This examination focuses on meanings, ideas and beliefs, and their implications for practice. While essentially intellectual, this examination has the practical aim of deepening the reader's comprehension of the operational models and approaches discussed in subsequent chapters of this volume. In so doing, it promotes better informed judgments about, and professionally sound utilization of these models. (This examination reflects the orientation that the intellectual and practical are inevitably and integrally linked [see Van Manen, 1977].)

THE IDIOSYNCRATIC SURVIVAL-RESPONSE FRAMEWORK

The first of the conceptual frameworks is distinct from the other two in that **teaching** and **teacher** are conceptualized as purely idiosyncratic. Within this framework the design, implementation and evaluation of the operational assistance model are not shaped or orchestrated by coherent images of these concepts. The meaning of these concepts can only be inferred from the specific assistance activities. Those meanings may vary widely, and are susceptible to contradiction. **Teacher** conceptualized as *technician* may be embedded in one set of assistance activities, while another set may communicate the image of **teacher** as *autonomous decision-maker*. Within

this framework, the concept **assistance** essentially means *responsiveness or reaction to expressed need*.

The operational assistance models that reflect this conceptual framework are often characterized by non-integrated components and actions. The collective assistance activities may reflect the entire continuum of the concepts **teacher** and **teaching**, from *laborer through *craftsman* to *professional and artistic decision-maker* (Mitchell & Kerchner, 1983). The response-oriented models may reduce **assistance** to "survival" tips and lack sufficient internal cohesion to exert long-term positive influence on the new teacher's professional practice. This lack of cohesion can lead to incongruent or contradictory assistance (e.g., suggestions for management and discipline that are highly teacher-centered and directed while suggestions related to instruction and learning activities promote student initiative, choice and self-regulation).

This idiosyncratic conceptual framework makes it impossible for the operational assistance effort to function as a coherent strategy for acculturating new teachers into the profession. This assistance model places responsibility for determining need and solution primarily, if not solely, with the new teachers themselves; arguably the least capable of making accurate assessments, by virtue of limited experience, high anxiety, and the natural confusions which are associated with the first teaching assignment. New teachers' expressed or felt needs are, all too often, directed at symptoms rather than issues or problems. While these expressions warrant a respectful hearing, the new teacher deserves the wisdom and insight of more experienced and, hopefully, more expert colleagues to assist in sorting through the complex phenomena of practice. The idiosyncratic conceptual framework and its attendant survival-response assistance models are ill-suited to assisting new teachers in developing a clear sense of "professional self" or in charting a coherent course of continuing professional growth.

* laborer — teaching is relegated to the presentation of standardized curriculum; craftsman — teaching requires the application of specialized techniques; professional and artistic decision-maker — careful analysis and diagnosis of the learning situation informs both the design and adaptation of instruction

THE TECHNICAL-INSTRUMENTAL FRAMEWORK

The second conceptual framework reflected in approaches to assisting new teachers is grounded in the positivist or empiricist epistemological tradition which emphasizes the paramount significance of overt observable behavior. The conceptions of **teaching**, **teacher**, and **assistance** embedded in this framework focus on demonstrable technical skill, precise performance, and observable behaviors. The process-product research of the past two decades which examined correlations between overt teacher behaviors and student achievement outcomes represents this tradition and these conceptions. This research has generated many of the prescriptions for teaching practice which are emphasized in new teacher assistance efforts based on this conceptual framework. Within this framework, **teaching** is *precise performance of clearly specified and sequenced behaviors*. **Teacher** is *performer, technician, implementor, executor*. Both conceptually and operationally, **assistance** in this framework relates to *technical training or retraining, the refinement or expansion of technically precise accurate performance* (see for example Mitchell & Kerchner, 1983; Van Manen, 1977). The prescriptions within this framework are characterized by minimal ambiguity with respect to behavior, and broad generic applicability across situations and subject areas.

Technical proficiency is the guiding image of this conceptual framework and the assistance models which follow from it. The substance and strategies of the operational models are aimed at improving or expanding precise performance and technical accuracy as ends in themselves.

This conceptual framework is strikingly distinct from the "survival-responsive" framework in its clearly articulated conceptions of **teaching** and **teacher**. These conceptions orchestrate the shape of the operational assistance models. To the extent that assistance based on this framework is responsive to new teachers' expressed needs, it is likely to first associate the expressed needs with research related to new teachers' performance and then translate them into terms or categories that can be addressed through strategies which emphasize technically precise behaviors, such as clearly sequenced steps of instruction or precise statements of consequences for behaviors in management.

Operational assistance models within this framework may differ from one another in terms of the specific performance areas they emphasize (e.g., management, instruction) or the particular research-based proficiency models they employ. Instructional assistance, for example, could in one effort emphasize direct instruction and employ the model embedded in the work of Brophy (1979), Brophy & Evertson (1977), Anderson, Evertson & Brophy (1979), Good & Grouws (1977, 1979). In another operational model, instructional assistance might emphasize the cooperative learning strategies reflected in the complex instruction model developed by Cohen (1983, 1987) and her associates. In either case, the emphasis of the assistance provided would be on the new teachers refining their technical performance proficiency with the particular model of instruction. Such would be the case, irrespective of the topic.

This conceptual framework and the operational assistance models which reflect it are highly congruent with the prevailing conception of teacher performance appraisal which relies on a checklist approach to teacher accountability and evaluations. This framework also is congruent with efforts to standardize curriculum, instruction, and instructional pacing throughout a school district or across the school districts of a state. Such state-level new teacher induction programs as those initiated in North Carolina, South Carolina, Florida, and Tennessee reflect this conceptual framework.

THE COMPLEX-INTELLECTUAL FRAMEWORK

The third conceptual framework for assisting new teachers reflects a similarly explicit conception of **teaching** and **teacher.** It is, however, considerably more complex and comprehensive than the technical instrumental framework, since it is rooted in the constructivist epistemological tradition which emphasizes human cognition, deliberation, and internally directed intentional action (see for example Ausubel, 1968; Shulman 1986, 1987; Giroux, 1988; Leinhardt, 1983; Stodolsky, 1988). Barnes (1989) succinctly summarizes this conception:

> . . . talking about teaching is analogous to describing a tapestry that has many threads of different colors woven into complicated textures and patterns. One can remove individual threads and examine them separately, but one cannot appreciate the complexity of the tapestry

without seeing how the threads are interwoven to create the whole cloth. . . . Teaching is seen as ambiguous and complex work requiring judgment, action, and the capacity to reflect and revise decisions on the basis of one's observations and insights. Sound teacher judgments must be rooted in deep understanding of teaching, learning, learners, and subject matter and how these factors interrelate in the teaching/learning process. (p. 13)

The focus of assistance for new teachers in this conceptual framework also is distinct from that represented in the other two frameworks. It would reflect that which Barnes recommends for preservice teacher preparation:

> . . . developing beginners' inclination and capacity to engage in the sort of intellectual dialogue and principled action required for effective teaching. . . . The capacities needed appear to be primarily intellectual in nature and do not merely result from training in the technical aspects of teaching. Rather, they involve learning to see, to judge, and to act appropriately in situations that cannot be precisely anticipated. (p. 17)

Technical proficiency, which constitutes the essence of the previous framework, is but one dimension of this framework. Here the technical dimension is embellished to encompass developing the teacher's understanding of the underlying assumptions and rationales, which in turn inform judgments about when and where to employ the technical skill.

Operational assistance efforts based on this conceptual framework emphasize structured reflection by the new teachers on their own teaching. This is done to affirm and hone intellectual disposition, orientation, judgment and such capabilities as synthesis and analysis without abstracting them from practice. The image of **teaching** embedded in this framework expresses these capacities as integral facets of both the conception itself and its practical representations. The teacher is intellectually engaged in this model. Both the capabilities and dispositions characteristic of that engagement are emphasized in the operational assistance effort.

Reflection is a prominent feature of assistance efforts grounded in this conceptual framework. Char-

acteristically, these assistance models engage new teachers in systematic, structured examination and analysis of their teaching practices. Such examinations focus on both the distinctive and interactive influences of learner characteristics, curricula, instructional approaches and materials, and school and classroom context. These exercises convey the centrality of informed judgment in action (see Gowin's (1981) discussion of "action as informed behavior") to this framework's conceptions of **teacher** and **teaching**. They also provide the new teachers with a strategic model for making sense of their practice (i.e., generating new understandings from practice) and then improving their practice and practical judgment on the basis of those understandings.

In practice these reflections might focus on analyzing curricula as representations of subject matter. "Is this reading curriculum phonics or grammar based?" "Is it literature?" "Is this mathematics curriculum really nothing more than computation?" Similarly, reflection might examine instructional strategies being used by the teachers as applications of learning theories and go on to explore their utility with a variety of distinct learnings (i.e., skills, concepts, facts, or values). These examples suggest that the conceptions of **teaching** and **teacher**, being conveyed through the assistance effort, encompass cognition, judgment, knowledge, and meaningful behavior or action. The whole of **teacher** or **teaching** is, in this conception, incomprehensible if individual dimensions are focused upon or emphasized in isolation.

THE CONCEPTUALLY ECLECTIC, CONCERNS-ORIENTED FRAMEWORK

The concerns-oriented framework does not conceptualize **teacher** in terms of categorical qualities (e.g., artisan, technician, reflective decision-maker) as do the **technical-instrumental** and **complex-intellectual** frameworks. This framework reflects the work of Fuller and Bown (1975) and more recently Berliner (1988), which defines **teacher** in relation to categories of concerns which occupy teachers' attention. According to Fuller and Bown these concerns follow a sequenced pattern: survival concerns, teaching situation concerns, pupil-oriented concerns. The allure of this framework for planners of assistance programs lies in its underlying notion of developmental stages through which teachers pass. Assistance programs based on this framework are likely to be structured around the posited sequence of concerns. Such programs begin with an emphasis on survival tips and a "get through the day" focus followed by activities that reflect a technical conception of **teaching**, then activities that suggest the teacher's need for reflective or intellectual engagement through activities requiring analysis, assessment and judgment.

A critical flaw in this framework is that, in conceptualizing **teacher** and **teaching**, it substitutes categories of concerns for defining or categorical characteristics of the concepts. Teachers and the concerns they have are not synonymous. Teachers' concerns are not their defining qualities. A further problem with this framework is that its premise of "sequenced" stages of concerns has been seriously challenged by research which has found teachers of varied experience levels to be concerned with issues from all three stage categories stipulated as sequential in this model (see for example Adams, Hutchinson, & Martray, 1980; Adams & Martray, 1981; Sitter & Lanier, 1982).

This sequence of concerns framework presents a smorgasbord of concepts of **teacher** and **teaching**, rather than a clearly oriented, coherently framed understanding of them. In accommodating multiple conceptions, it fails to assess and address the conflicting or contradictory features inherent in the different conceptualizations and in their implications for practice. It can easily engender in new teachers a muddled sense of what it means to be a teacher or to teach. Assistance approaches based on this framework provide little direction to new teachers for structuring, comprehending and intelligently acting on new experiences. Their appeal lies in their appearance of being grounded in research or theory or both.

Discussion

In both the **technical-instrumental** and the **complex-intellectual** frameworks, the conceptions of **teaching** and **teacher** deliberately shape the substance and strategies of the operational assistance efforts. At the same time, these assistance efforts serve to acculturate new teachers to teaching and to being teachers in terms of the embedded conceptions. In other words, the assistance efforts reflect and communicate deliberate meaning of **teaching** and **teacher** to the neophytes. No such intentional image imprinting is evident in the **survival-response** framework. There very likely is an image communicated —

one that is fuzzy and somewhat incoherent. The sequence of concerns-oriented framework suggests progressively changing conceptions of **teaching** and **teacher** based on preoccupying concerns. As was discussed above, the whole premise of this framework is both conceptually and empirically suspect.

The relationship between conceptual frameworks and operational assistance efforts is essentially reciprocal. While the conceptual framework provides an orientation and initial direction and shaping influence on the operational model, once the effort is underway it will influence modifications, clarification and embellishments of the framework. The absence of congruence between the conceptual framework and the strategies employed in the operational model would likely reduce the conceptual framework to mere rhetoric. The absence of this congruence also can result in less coherent and, therefore, less effective operational models.

As Van Manen (1977) argues, conceptions are as much orientations — ways of looking at things — as they are classifying or definitional categories. Murray's (1989) observation regarding research, "Basically researchers search only for what they believe exists," also has an analog in this discussion. What is believed about **teacher** and **teaching** influences the commitment to and shape of operational assistance to new teachers. Such beliefs are always imbedded in practical actions whether tacitly or deliberately. Conceptual analysis is, therefore, a critically practical component of assistance effort design and implementation.

Any number of forces can influence the conceptual and practical shape of new teacher assistance efforts. For example, in instances where states (legislatures or administrative agencies) serve as catalysts and funding sources for assistance efforts as part of their teacher performance appraisal agendas, the conceptual framework of the assistance models will reflect that of the agenda. Other influential forces are the expertise and orientations of individuals involved in designing and implementing the assistance effort and perhaps the institutions those individuals represent. This is not to say that involvement by particular groups necessarily predetermines either the conceptual framework or the operational model of the assistance effort. The new teachers who participate in the assistance program are likely to influence its shape and focus. How much influence any of these forces has depends on how roles are defined and perceived, whether constructive candor can be generated and sustained among participants and whether there is an inclination and effort to regularly monitor alignment between the conceptual framework and the operative dimensions of the assistance effort.

This chapter offers a brief summary of four conceptual frameworks associated with initiatives to assist new teachers. It also provides a summary of how those frameworks are reflected in, influence, or shape operational models of assistance to new teachers. It briefly identifies key factors which may influence the reciprocal relationship between conceptual frameworks and practical assistance efforts.

The basic proposition is that conceptualizations of **teacher**, **teaching**, and **assistance** play very active and directive though sometimes subtle roles in shaping efforts to assist and acculturate new teachers into the profession. The fact that these conceptualizations are often more tacit than explicit does not diminish or negate their influence.

Comprehending the conceptual frameworks embedded in assistance efforts and being more explicit about the frameworks as they influence those efforts are of crucial importance. They make us critical and therefore better informed consumers of previously developed assistance models. They are essential to establishing accurate and valid standards or criteria for assessing utility, impact and effectiveness of such efforts. For the reader of this volume, the conceptual frameworks may be either illuminating guides or focusing lenses through which to consider the book's ideas, descriptions, and discussions.

REFERENCES

Adams, R., & Martray, C. (1981). *Teacher development: A study of factors related to teacher concerns for pre, beginning, and experienced teachers.* Paper presented at the annual meeting of the American Research Association, Los Angeles.

Adams, R., Hutchinson, S., & Martray, C. (1980). *A developmental study of teacher concerns across time.* Paper presented at the annual meeting of the American Research Association, Boston.

Anderson, L.M., Evertson, C.M., & Brophy, J.E. (1979). An experimental study of effective teaching in first-grade reading groups. *The Elementary School Journal*, 193-222.

Ausubel, D.P. (1968). *Educational psychology: A cognitive view.* New York: Holt, Rinehard and Winston.

Barnes, H. (1989). Structuring knowledge for beginning teachers. In M.C. Reynolds (Ed.), *Knowledge base for the beginning teacher.* New York: Pergamon Press.

Berliner, D. (1988). Expert-novice differences in perceiving and processing visual classroom information. *Journal of Teacher Education*, 39(3).

Brophy, J.E. & Evertson, C.M. (1977). Teacher behavior and student learning in second and third grades. In G.D. Borich (Ed.), *The appraisal of teaching: Concepts and process* (pp. 79-95). Reading, MA: Addison-Wesley.

Brophy, J.E. (1979). Teacher behavior and its effects. *Journal of Educational Psychology*, 71, 733-750.

Cohen, E.G. (1983). Talking and working together: Status, interaction and learning. In P. Peterson and L.C. Wilkinson (Eds.), *Instructional groups in the classroom: Organization and processes.* New York: Academic Press.

Cohen, E.G. (1987). *Designing groupwork: Strategies for heterogeneous classrooms.* New York: Teachers College Press.

Fuller, F. & Bown, O. (1975). Becoming a teacher. In K. Ryan (Ed.), *Teacher education.* The 74th Yearbook of the National Society for the Study of Education, Part II. Chicago: University of Chicago Press.

Giroux, H. (1988). *Teachers as intellectuals: toward a critical pedagogy of learning.* Granby, MA: Bergin and Garvey Publishers, Inc.

Good, T.L., & Grouws, D.A. (1977). Teaching effects: A process-product study in fourth grade mathematics classrooms. *Journal of Teacher Education*, 28,(3).

Good, T.L. (1979). Teacher effectiveness in the elementary school. *Journal of Teacher Education*, 30(2).

Gowin, D. (1981). *Educating*. Ithaca, NY: Cornell University Press.

Leinhardt, G. (1983). Novice and expert knowledge of individual students' achievement. *Educational Psychologist*, 18, 165-79.

Mitchell & Kerchner. (1983). In Shulman and Sykes (Eds.), *Handbook of teaching and policy*, New York: Longman.

Murray, F. (1989). Explanations in education. In M.C. Reynolds (Ed.), *Knowledge base for the beginning teacher*. New York: Pergamon Press.

Shulman, L.S. (1986). Those who understand: Knowledge growth in teaching. *Educational Researcher*, 15(2), 4-14.

Shulman, L.S. (1987). Knowledge and teaching: Foundations of the new reform. *Harvard Educational Review*, 57(1), 1-22.

Sitter, J., & Lanier, P. (1982). *Student teaching: A stage in the development of a teacher?* Paper presented at the annual meeting of the American Research Association, New York.

Stodolsky, S. (1988). *The subject matters*. Chicago, IL: University of Chicago Press.

Van Manen, M. (1977). Linking ways of knowing with ways of being practical. *Curriculum Inquiry* 6:3, 205-228.

Chapter 3

Content and Strategies for Assisting New Teachers

Diane S. Murphy
San Diego State University

Katherine K. Merseth
University of California, Riverside

Ann I. Morey
San Diego State University

Diane S. Murphy
San Diego State University

Katherine K. Merseth
University of California, Riverside

Ann I. Morey
San Diego State University

A Scenario of Failure... and New Stories of Success

I am a new teacher, which means I am taking over an empty classroom, right? When I walk in the classroom door, it is bare. There is not a piece of paper, a pencil! There are no erasers! No chalk! No teacher's guides! No textbooks! I am lucky if there are chairs and tables and desks. I might not even have a garbage can, but if I do, it is probably full because the custodian did not enter that room since the former teacher left in June. That is what I enter into. If I am lucky, it is two or three days before the kids arrive. If I am typical, it's three hours before the kids arrive because I got hired just after school started when district personnel knew they had enough kids to need me. If I am really unlucky, it's two weeks after the kids arrive and I am getting all the kids who do not want to be there because they are leaving their buddies from classes they were in before I came.

Second, no one tells me where to get the books, papers, crayons, and erasers I need. Finally, I get brave enough to interrupt a person, who I know does not want to be interrupted, and she says: "Go down and ask the secretary in the principal's office where the bookroom is." Now in most schools, when I arrive at the bookroom, there is a clerk there with a thousand forms to fill out and no books on the shelf . . . because all you experienced people (you, who have had the privilege of being in that school if you wanted to for the last two weeks) have been popping in and and grabbing every new book that came in the door. You have them in your classroom! So what is left are the dregs that nobody else wants. I don't know if they are good books or bad books. I don't even know if they are appropriate to the kids I am going to teach; and nobody is there to help me make that decision. I go to the supply room for paper, pencils, and crayons. If I'm lucky there are some left. If not, all the teachers who are experienced and have been there already have taken everything that came in the first supply shipment. Here I sit. The kids arrive tomorrow morning. I don't know what I am going to do. If I had any plan from my preservice training, it at least required paper, pencils, and books!

Now, here's the other thing that happens in a typical California classroom: the next day kids from at least three if not five different ethnic backgrounds walk into my room. Several of these children do not speak English. Regardless of how good my preservice preparation was, it could not have prepared me for this! [Taken from interviews with new teachers — reported by Beatrice A. Ward, 1989]

This unfortunate scenario is the experience of many novice California teachers. However, success stories are beginning to surface as well, largely due to beginning teacher support programs now being piloted in the state. Consider the words of two new teachers who have had advisors assigned to assist them at their school sites:

My start-up partner was (and is) incredible! We began working together during the last part of summer vacation and she was always available for questions, ideas, support and an occasional shoulder to cry on. We went over my discipline plan, classroom setting and organization, my lesson plans, etc. Many times we stayed at school through the dinner hour discussing and working on school projects. I feel very close to her and know I can go to her with my needs. She always has treated me as an equal and I will always be grateful for her assistance. [A secondary language arts teacher.]

I needed to be supported emotionally and advised as to the school day's 'ebb and flow.' All questions I may have had concerning materials, texts, etc. were answered. My "buddy" often came to my room for a drop-in visit and commented positively on what she saw. She shared her ideas and materials willingly and was excited about mine. [A combination 1st/2nd grade teacher.]

Their experiences are cause for hope: hope that the scenario of failure will be replaced by stories of success as the effects of beginning teacher programs for a few become the norm for the profession.

This chapter is designed to provide information on the content and strategies of assistance that have helped to create these stories of success within California. The information presented reflects the shared knowledge and experience of beginning teacher project leaders who attended the statewide invitational workshops on beginning teacher programs. At the workshops, "content of assistance" was defined as the subject matter that is emphasized in beginning teacher programs. "Strategies of assistance" were defined as ways that assistance is delivered, including who provides the assistance and how it is provided. The chapter has been organized to identify the content and strategies that have been highly emphasized in California programs, and to illustrate both the similarity and diversity of program assistance. It describes assistance for starting the school year as well as for improving instructional performance throughout the first year. The chapter also suggests adaptations for large geographical regions, multicultural school settings, year-round education, and secondary school programs.

DETERMINING THE CONTENT OF BEGINNING TEACHER PROGRAMS

Major tasks confronting planners of new teacher assistance are determining program content and establishing priorities. An assessment of new teacher needs is a valuable way to learn new teachers' perceptions of their situation. However, new teachers have a limited experience base for analyzing the types of assistance they may need. Thus, it is important to incorporate the informed knowledge of researchers and practitioners who understand the needs of new teachers within the broader context of the profession in planning an assistance program. There is a growing body of literature which should be explored in this process, including *Knowledge Base for the Beginning Teacher* (1989), a recent publication by the American Association of Colleges for Teacher Education. In addition, prospective leaders can learn from the combined knowledge of those currently implementing new teacher programs.

In order to identify the content areas and emphases of new teacher programs within California, the 66 project leaders at The Invitational Workshop on Beginning Teacher Programs in San Diego were asked to indicate the degree of emphasis placed on specific content areas in their 1988-89 programs and whether they intended to retain or modify these emphases in 1989-90. Beginning the list of content areas to which participants responded were the 10 most frequently cited new teacher problems identified in Veenman's (1984) review of studies on beginning teacher needs. Other areas frequently addressed

FIGURE 1
DEGREE OF EMPHASIS IN ASSISTANCE

Please rate the degree of emphasis in assistance (low—>high) that is currently provided in your project (what is) and indicate your intent to retain or modify that emphasis as you plan for next year (what will be). Rate only those areas you include or intend to include as part of your project. Leave the others blank.

What Is low —> high		Emphasis in Assistance	What Will Be low —> high
1 2 3 4 5	1)	Classroom discipline	1 2 3 4 5
1 2 3 4 5	2)	Motivating students	1 2 3 4 5
1 2 3 4 5	3)	Dealing with individual student differences	1 2 3 4 5
1 2 3 4 5	4)	Assessing students' work	1 2 3 4 5
1 2 3 4 5	5)	Relations with parents	1 2 3 4 5
1 2 3 4 5	6)	Organization of class work	1 2 3 4 5
1 2 3 4 5	7)	Materials and supplies	1 2 3 4 5
1 2 3 4 5	8)	Dealing with problems of individual students	1 2 3 4 5
1 2 3 4 5	9)	Balancing heavy teaching loads & preparation time	1 2 3 4 5
1 2 3 4 5	10)	Colleague relations	1 2 3 4 5
1 2 3 4 5	11)	Psychological support	1 2 3 4 5
1 2 3 4 5	12)	Coping with isolation	1 2 3 4 5
1 2 3 4 5	13)	District related issues	1 2 3 4 5
1 2 3 4 5	14)	Standardized testing	1 2 3 4 5
1 2 3 4 5	15)	Stress management	1 2 3 4 5
1 2 3 4 5	16)	Curriculum issues	1 2 3 4 5
1 2 3 4 5	17)	Record keeping	1 2 3 4 5
1 2 3 4 5	18)	Procedures for referrals	1 2 3 4 5
1 2 3 4 5	19)	Time management	1 2 3 4 5
1 2 3 4 5	20)	Professional growth plans	1 2 3 4 5
1 2 3 4 5	21)	Preparing for substitutes	1 2 3 4 5
1 2 3 4 5	22)		1 2 3 4 5
1 2 3 4 5	23)		1 2 3 4 5
1 2 3 4 5	24)		1 2 3 4 5
1 2 3 4 5	25)		1 2 3 4 5

by new teacher programs were added to the list. (See Figure 1.)

The highly emphasized content areas designated by a majority of the leaders who implemented programs in 1988-89 are presented in ranked order of response:

Content highly emphasized in 1988-89

- **psychological support**
- **curriculum issues**
- **classroom discipline**
- **colleague relations**
- **relations with parents**

It is interesting to note that two of these areas — psychological support and curriculum issues — were not among those identified in the Veenman review (1984).

The content areas that most of these respondents planned to highly emphasize in 1989-1990 include these five plus an additional 11 topics.

Content highly emphasized in 1989-90

- motivating students
- **classroom discipline**
- organization of classwork
- dealing with individual student differences
- **relations with parents**
- **colleague relations**

- **psychological support**
- coping with isolation
- time management
- professional growth planning
- **curriculum issues**
- dealing with problems of individual students
- balancing heavy teaching loads and preparation
- stress management
- materials and supplies
- preparation for substitutes

It is not surprising that classroom discipline is an important content area in most new teacher programs. Discipline was identified in Veenman's study (1984) as the primary problem of new teachers. The content listing shows that programs in California have underscored this common need. However, it is particularly interesting to note that content associated with motivating students is the area in which most programs intend to intensify assistance in the second year of implementation. Perhaps the relationship between student behavior and student motivation for learning is being recognized and efforts to emphasize this relationship are being incorporated as induction programs become more sophisticated in addressing new teacher needs.

The projected expansion in content focus and emphasis of assistance in programs within California could be attributed to various factors:

- refinement of the perceived needs of new teachers during the initial year of program implementation

- redesign of programs based on a reflective analysis of the strengths and limitations of the original program design and implementation

- networking between projects about ways to enhance assistance

- feeling of greater competence by the project leaders, facilitating the introduction of a wider range of subjects following the initial year of implementation.

But whatever is prompting the changes, the diversity of topics listed reflects the complex challenge confronting those who would attempt to support and assist new teachers.

FIGURE 2
RANKS

Strategy of Assistance	Project leaders	Beginning Teachers CANTP	NTRP
Money for classroom set-up expense	1.5	1	5
Help in their classrooms provided by experienced teachers	1.5	4	1
Observe expert teachers	3	2.5	4
Attend mentor teacher presentations	5	5	7
Talk with other new teachers	5	7	2
Demonstration lessons taught in the new teacher's classroom	5	6	6
Support and guidance from the principal	7	2.5	3
To attend educational conferences of their choice	8	9	9
To attend workshops	9.5	8	8
Formal university coursework on a wide range of classroom management and curriculum concerns.	9.5	10	10

Individually ranked scores under each strategy of assistance were summed and then divided by the number of respondents in order to determine a ranked order of response for the project leaders and each of the new teachers groups.

DETERMINING STRATEGIES OF ASSISTANCE

Many strategies are available to assist beginning teachers. Similar to determining content, new teacher needs and/or wants are only one criterion on which selection of strategies should be based. However, identifying the preferences of novice teachers can be an important ingredient in program design. At the invitational workshop, project leaders were asked to rank 10 strategies in the order they felt would reflect what new teachers want most in an induction program. In addition, participants in one of the California New Teacher Projects (CANTP) and one of the state's Inner-City New Teacher Retention Projects (NTRP) were asked to rank the same list. (See Figure 2.)

The consensus across all three groups is that new teachers much prefer assistance that is immediate and is provided at the school site. Given the time constraints and contextual needs associated with the first year of teaching, workshops, conferences, and formal coursework were not highly rated.

Interestingly, both new teacher groups ranked support from the principal among their top three preferences, while project directors ranked principal support seventh. It may be that project directors tend to minimize the significant role principals play in the experiences of new teachers. This significance may pertain to the existing evaluation system and the perceived (or real) power of the principal within the school setting.

The variation in responses between new teacher groups suggests that the structures of assistance provided may have a significant influence on which type is valued. "Talking with other new teachers" was ranked second by the New Teacher Retention Project and seventh by the California New Teacher Project. The Retention program requires weekly meetings of small cluster groups of new teachers (approximately six teachers per group) as compared to optional monthly large group new teacher meetings in the New Teacher Project model. The higher rating from Retention project teachers may reflect the satisfaction of relationships that resulted from the clustering process and its continuity. Similarly, the teachers who gave a high ranking to "money for classroom set-up expense" had been matched with a start-up partner who was encouraged to take them shopping at the beginning of the school year and help them make appropriate selections of instructional materials. The other group of teachers received only written and oral instructions on how to purchase materials. Most of the second group did not use the stipend until late in the school-year.

It should be noted that formalized university coursework is ranked last by all respondents. Feedback from discussion groups at both conferences indi-

cates that assistance offered through coursework is more valued if modifications are made in the formalized structures of masters level coursework. For example, in some projects, new teachers and advisors have taken classes together and have engaged in action research which specifically applies to their particular school setting. San Diego State University incorporated structures to promote reflective analysis of an individual's teaching experience through the use of critical incident summaries and case reports. New teachers spend 10 minutes of each class session writing about a critical experience (positive or negative) of the past week. These accounts help focus individual thought and prompt small cluster group discussion guided by a university professor. The accounts are developed into case reports by incorporating descriptions of contextual factors and an analysis of all the elements of the experience. The personally relevant nature of the writing and the insights derived from the discussions among teacher educators and new teacher colleagues tend to minimize the burden of university coursework added to an already challenging schedule.

Similarity and Diversity of Support for New Teachers Within California

Similarities exist in the types of beginning teacher support in California state-funded pilot projects. Most programs include: 1) assigning an experienced teacher/faculty member to assist new teachers; 2) training for new teachers; 3) new teacher support groups; and 4) stipends for classroom set-up. But, by design, there is significant variation in the intensity of assistance. Projects are funded at different levels. Projects fund $500 to $5,000 per new teacher so that evaluators can analyze the impact of various levels of assistance on the attainment of induction goals. The most intense assistance, though relatively very expensive, may be the most cost-effective option if the intensity results in distinguishable improvement in new teacher performance and retention. Figure 3 describes four types of assistance; the strategies listed under each illustrate the variation in design and intensity among the projects.

ASSISTANCE FOR BEGINNING THE SCHOOL YEAR

Research indicates that even the most competent student teachers tend to experience feelings of inadequacy and incompetence at the beginning of the first year of professional practice (Murphy, 1988).

FIGURE 3
TYPES OF ASSISTANCE

Assignment of an Experienced Advisor

Intensive Assistance
Full-time Advisor (1:12 ratio)
In-class assistance weekly
(e.g., 3 hrs.)

Moderate Assistance
Assigned school site advisor
Release days to work together

Minimal Assistance
Assigned school site advisor
No structures for working
together during school time

Training for the New Teacher

Intensive Assistance
Required/paid training for
new and assisting teachers
(can include release days)

Moderate Assistance
Required/paid training for
new teachers
Training optional for advisors

Minimal Assistance
Voluntary attendance at
training for new and assisting
teachers (no monetary
compensation)

New Teacher Support Groups

Intensive Assistance
Regularly scheduled site-
based meetings with
knowledgeable theorists
and practitioners

Moderate Assistance
Structured meetings with advisors
who have limited background in
theory and/or practice

Minimal Assistance
Support and interaction
limited to other new teachers
(no guidance from
experienced educators)

Stipends for Classroom Set-up

Intensive Assistance
$500-$1000

Moderate Assistance
$200-$300

Minimal Assistance
$100 or less

Evertson (1989) clarifies why the need for start-up assistance is so pervasive among beginning teachers:

> The preservice teacher has rarely observed and rarely participated in the construction of a world of learning; rather, he or she has generally entered such a world in midstream, expecting to fit in and preserve the status quo of the classroom. Thus, how to begin is an issue that falls between the cracks of the preservice world and the world of the professional teacher. (p. 59)

The challenge of providing adequate assistance in a typically inadequate amount of time is complicated by the fact that beginning-of-the-year assistance must incorporate information on such diverse elements as: 1) district and school site orientation; 2) classroom set-up; 3) acquisition and organization of instructional materials and supplies; and 4) creating a learning environment. Strategies included in this section are being used by California educators actively engaged in start-up assistance for new teachers. To be effective, start up strategies must include ways to promote motivation, information, and accountability for assigned advisors as well as ideas for

integrating the new teacher into the profession. California educators are using the following:

Hiring Practices. In some districts, experienced grade level or departmental personnel become actively involved in the interview and selection process and assume responsibility for assisting the new teacher in order to support and justify their selection. They also provide input to the principal as to who might make the best match as an advisor for the new teacher.

Advisor Assignment. It is easier to ask for the help of experienced educators if the new teacher and other project participants know that assisting roles have been formally assigned to advisors. To the extent possible, advisor assignment is made upon hiring. Advisors are given explicit information about role expectations. A good advisor/new teacher match is more likely if the advisor is accessible at the school site, has the same grade level expertise, is strong in classroom management and discipline, is sensitive to the psychological needs of new teachers, and is committed to providing the necessary time for assisting a new teacher.

Social Gatherings. Several projects host social events such as luncheons where new teachers and their advisors meet in an informal setting. Frequently, other school-site, district, and university personnel attend.

Intensive Workshops/Conferences. Some districts offer one-week or even longer conferences exploring topics important to new and veteran teachers. For example, one site has a Summer Institute for advisors and new teachers. It provides several weeks of immersion on a topic, such as instructional strategies for diverse classrooms. Another district sponsors a Professional Development Center where new teachers spend a week prior to the start of school. They get acquainted with other teachers in the school and district; and together new and experienced teachers review the school curriculum, discuss seating arrangements, bulletin boards, and classroom management.

Project Orientation. The projects use a variety of formats to orient new teachers and other personnel to the project. Some districts orient new teachers, principals, and other assisting personnel in one large group meeting so that all participants can hear the same information, have the same expectations, and provide an accountability check on each other for assistance offered and received.

Handbook for New Teachers. A handbook is a helpful tool that can facilitate orientation to the project, district, and school site. Some handbooks state expectations for professional growth and present the project's conceptual basis. One handbook presents five different steps to be mastered before the school year begins, and is the major sourcebook for workshops prior to classes. Some handbooks also include pertinent information that the new teacher is too overwhelmed to absorb in an orientation meeting. They may also serve as directories for local and district resources, or as guides for assisting educators.

One-on-One. Advisors visit the new teacher's classroom and help them set it up. They help the teacher obtain curriculum materials and generally get oriented to the school and its resources (or lack thereof).

Stipends for Classroom Set-up and Other Purposes. Since beginning teachers do not have the inventory of materials that experienced teachers accumulate, they receive stipends to offset costs of materials needed to create a learning environment. Stipends generally range from $100 to $500.

New Teacher Desk Kit. The district warehouse provides a kit of predetermined, standard desk materials (gradebook, stapler, scissors, etc.) for each grade level. Each grade level kit has a specific order number so that delivery can be arranged as soon as a new teacher is hired.

Ordering Classroom Materials and Supplies. Principals replacing retiring or transferring teachers request that those teachers order class sets of materials (texts, papers, etc.) as if they would be returning so that their replacements do not end up with shortages and/or the "dregs" of the district.

School and Neighborhood Tour. A welcoming/orientation strategy could include a tour of the school to introduce new teachers to personnel as well as show them all the things that experienced teachers already know (e.g., cubbyholes of supplies). If the tour includes the neighborhood, the new teacher can gain insights into many factors affecting the children who live there.

Late-hire Contingency Plan. A contingency plan for late hires is developed in conjunction with the beginning teacher program offerings for all new teachers. This plan reflects the practical time and personnel constraints associated with late hiring. If checklists for assistance have been formulated in advance, alternative approaches can be anticipated and incorporated.

Video-tapes of school start-up. Video-tapes of outstanding teachers at work in the first week of school have proven helpful to new teachers who have never participated in creating a learning environment. Tapes for each grade level can be developed and duplicated for check-out. These can be used as a focus of grade level new teacher group meetings, advisor/new teacher conferencing, or individual viewing.

Shadowing. To capitalize on a new teacher's intrinsic motivation to prepare for school, districts prepare a list of experienced teachers who are willing to have a new teacher shadow them during the instructional day. Available dates are determined and disseminated to new hires. Depending on the hiring date, shadowing occurs in the spring, summer or fall. In schools operating on a year-round schedule, staggered start-up dates make this easier. For new teachers hired after school begins, a shadowing experience lasting one day to one week could be required as an alternative to hiring a teacher for immediate placement.

Assistance for Improving Instructional Performance

The prospectus for the American Association of Colleges for Teacher Education's, *Knowledge Base for the Beginning Teacher*, asserts:

> Knowledgeable teachers are not technicians, but professionals — worthy and able to make decisions and plans based on principled knowledge that is adapted to the particulars of their teaching situation, their students, their unique experience and their own special insights, self-knowledge, values and commitments (Gardner, 1989).

Helping new teachers improve instructional performance is the essence of a quality beginning teacher program. Getting acclimated to a new setting and position is vital but it is merely a foundation for the more complex challenge of becoming an effective and professional teacher. Ideally, the process of assisting new teachers to become professional begins in teacher preparation and extends into the initial years of teaching. It requires the establishment of structures to help integrate the experiential wisdom of expert teachers, the knowledge gained at the university and the innovative and exploratory ideas of novice teachers.

The threats to attainment are the constraints of time, training, and precedent. Nevertheless, the goal of improving instructional performance must remain central to the content and strategies associated with new teacher assistance. Structures must be developed that will create time for assistance; expert educators should be trained in ways to effectively assist novice teachers; and expectations for induction must be clearly established within the profession. The strategies presented in this section are among those being used by project leaders who are currently engaged in implementing programs to reach the goal of improving the instructional performance of beginning teachers.

Workshops, Conferences, and Other Meetings. A variety of formats can be used for this type of staff development, including after-school workshops, full or partial release days, weekend events, and local, state and national conferences. Through these activities, new teachers can gain knowledge, understanding, and skills that will help them in a range of areas such as parent conferences, back-to-school-night, grading and record-keeping, effective teaching, different instructional strategies, bilingual education, specific curriculum areas, and teaching and learning in ethnically diverse classrooms. These activities, particularly when in the form of attendance at professional seminars and conferences, can also provide acculturation into the profession.

Curriculum Forums and Follow-up Meetings. Several projects offer day-long forums to enhance content knowledge in core curriculum areas and to promote skill in instructional planning and delivery. Follow-up meetings encourage implementation of instructional strategies and provide opportunities to raise questions and share ideas and experiences. When school site advisors are able to attend the same forums and follow-up meetings, support in planning for specific contextual and grade level concerns can be more effectively integrated.

University Courses for Beginning Teachers. University coursework is designed especially for new teachers. Using a variety of formats (e.g., seminars, critical incident writing and analysis, lectures) courses have included topics ranging from stress management, classroom management, and multicultural education to parent relations. Courses also include components on second language acquisition, instructional strategies, and teaching in the content areas.

Setting up for Substitutes. The work of preparing for and, in some cases, "making up for" a substitute can often negate the benefits of a release day inservice for improving instruction. One solution is to suspend continuity of instruction for a day and allow substitutes, prepared with special grade level materials which have been approved by district curriculum coordinators, to teach content that they have perfected and that is worthy of interrupting the established sequence of instruction.

Integration of Research Literature into Practice. New teachers, veteran teachers, and university faculty review the research literature on relevant topics and use it to guide classroom practice and to develop professional growth activities for new teachers. Specific projects have used research findings to structure activities on classroom management, effective schools, and such topics as the teaching of reading, math, science, and cooperative education.

Cluster Groups. Groups of six to eight new teachers meet regularly with a university faculty member or experienced teacher to promote acculturation, the development of problem-solving skills, reflective analysis, and expertise in identified areas.

Critical Incident Summaries. New teachers meet weekly and do a brief writing session on an incident (positive or negative) that occurred at their school. The process of writing helps new teachers formulate and articulate their own thoughts and insights. Small groups facilitated by a veteran teacher or university faculty member discuss some of the "incidents" to promote understanding, reflective thinking, and peer problem-solving.

Case Studies. Published case studies are a useful tool to engage new teachers in analyzing situations and promoting professional growth. In one project, new teachers also develop their own case studies which are reviewed by a university faculty member and are discussed in group meetings.

Journals. Like critical incident summaries and case studies, journal writing is another useful mode of self-examination and can lead to clarification of issues, a habit of reflection, and skill at problem solving.

Clinical Supervision. Advisors and university faculty clinically supervise the new teacher in the classroom. Preconferences, classroom observations, and post-conferences characterize this strategy in which new teachers identify change targets and write professional development goals.

Lesson Observations and Conferencing. Various kinds of observation are incorporated, depending on the objective of assistance. The new teacher observes experienced teachers to become aware of alternative styles and strategies. Or the advisor and the novice teacher observe another teacher. In the latter case, the advisor guides the new teacher in a reflective analysis of the instructional process.

Assess to Assist. Strategies of observation must be linked to the concept that becoming a teacher is a process and that assessment is the foundation for assistance. In some projects, structures for self-assessment are incorporated with other forms of formative evaluation (e.g., cognitive coaching and reflective supervision). Visual and auditory tapes with written guidelines to promote diagnosis and analysis are used by new teachers in consultation with experienced educators.

Team Teaching. A potentially less threatening strategy than structured teacher observation is team teaching, in which classes are combined for some units and novice and veteran teachers collaboratively plan, teach, and evaluate the instructional experience.

Video Tapes. Video tapes are produced by university faculty and district personnel as well as commercial enterprises. These tapes can assist new teachers in dealing with teaching situations.

Second-year Teachers as Buddies. Second-year teachers are invited to activities with first-year teachers. Because they can identify closely with the new teachers, they can provide assurance, insights, and practical information. This structured interaction also has proven a vehicle for the continued professional growth of second-year teachers.

Newsletters. Project newsletters are a way to introduce the new teachers, report project information and cover topics of interest.

Help-Line. New teachers discuss matters with a public school teacher, retired teacher, principal and/or university professor, all available by telephone. In one project, Help-Line members visit new teachers' classrooms and provide on-site assistance.

Team Approach to Assistance. A team of educators works with a specific teacher throughout the year. The team often consists of an administrator, a resource teacher, an experienced grade-level teacher, and a university professor.

Professional Growth Planning. Since 1985, credentialed new teachers in California must develop an individualized professional growth plan and accumulate a minimum of 150 hours of participation in activities related to targeted growth goals within five years of receiving the initial credential in order to renew the Professional Clear Teaching Credential. Several new teacher programs train experienced educators to serve as professional growth advisors and provide inservices within the beginning teacher program that directly correlate with the new teacher's need to identify goals and develop a plan.

ADAPTING ASSISTANCE FOR SPECIFIC SITUATIONS

The content and assistance of new teacher programs must be adapted to the unique settings in which new teachers begin their teaching careers. Adaptations for specific situations which will be discussed in this section are presented under the following topics: 1) distance assistance: supporting new teachers electronically; 2) year-round education assistance; 3) assistance in multicultural school settings; and 4) secondary level assistance.

Distance Assistance: Supporting New Teachers Electronically

Some California projects are designed to assist beginning teachers and their advisors over large geographical regions. Some use interactive video and cable television. Others provide assistance through an interactive network of personal computers which can electronically transfer text messages from one person to another or to a group of individuals. An example of such a program is the Beginning Teacher Computer Network which was initiated at the Harvard Graduate School of Education.

Assistance delivered by an interactive computer network connects teachers who are assigned to even the most remote locations. According to the Harvard model, electronic support differs in two important respects from typical assistance programs: first, rather than one advisor to one advisee, all the participants give advice to each other, resulting in a model of professional development that defines an advisor as a collection of individuals rather than one person; second, the vast majority of members are colleagues of equal status, negating much of the expert-novice interaction of most assistance programs. With the exception of the university participants and occasional invited guests, all of the comments, advice and professional support given to the first year teachers come from other first year teachers. This equal status of nearly all the members causes the network to resemble peer coaching models of staff development.

Network conversations range widely, frequently moving from a specific example or question to more general exchanges or consideration of principles. As an example, one Network message exchange initially focused on classroom management skills, i.e., how to keep student chattering under control. This stimulated five somewhat prescriptive peer responses. Responses moved within a few days to a broader consideration of student motivation and the purposes of education. The conversation began to diverge after the following comment by one of the beginning teachers: "A lot of this discussion has been on order and only a little bit of it is on what that order should serve. . . . Order isn't what teaching is about." One week later, a junior high science teacher responded with the message: "It is not so much the algebra, biology, and writing that we teach, it is the feeling of self-worth and confidence. . . ." This launched the electronic group discussion into a consideration of personal priorities in teaching and a debate about the relative importance of "character development" and "purer academics."

Because the network collectively represents not one, but a wide range of teaching environments, there exists a "sieve of neutrality" with regard to local context knowledge. This local detachment, combined with multiple perspectives of different individuals from diverse subject matter fields, generalizes the specific incident or situation to a higher level of abstraction. Networking, with its focus on the content of the message and not on the local culture, seems to foster the ability of novices to perceive more broadly and more generally, helping them gain perspectives on their own teaching and on the teaching of others. Used in conjunction with a school site advisor who assists with important local context concerns, the network may well stimulate a level of reflection not often found in teacher education or staff development programs.

While experienced educators know that many first-year teachers will experience a remarkably similar set of problems regardless of their school or classroom location, novices often do not have this perspective. They frequently feel that they are the "only ones" with discipline issues, management problems or questions about the purposes of education. The network provides novice teachers with a means to share a teaching experience or a thought at any hour of the day or night. This connectedness, providing continuity from their training experiences as well as contact with each other, helps break down the sense of isolation that is particularly devastating to beginners. One participant observed, "Hearing about other people's problems made me feel less alone. Those conversations let me know it wasn't just me."

The question is often asked: Is assistance through a computer network expensive? Thirty-eight Beginning Teacher Computer Network participants reported an average monthly usage rate of 6.1 hours per person per month for a total of 61 hours for the year. Costs to implement the system are derived from the capital expenditures for the host equipment, telephone line charges, and technical personnel to maintain the system. The proliferation of computers in schools makes it possible for participants to use these computers to participate. Total Network expenditures were $12,750 for the 1987-88 academic year, resulting in a cost per hour of use of $5.50. In subsequent years, assuming the same participation rates and cohort size, the annual cost drops to approximately $6000 resulting in an hourly rate of $2.91 because equipment is re-used and no further equipment purchases are necessary.

Noting that the average number of hours logged by participants closely resembles the number of contact hours for a one semester university course, this technology offers a pragmatic and relatively low cost means for universities to provide formal support to beginning teacher graduates. As in their university preservice teacher education experience, teachers now gather electronically across thousands of miles to consider a specific situation, problem or case. Only now the "grist" or material for discussion is not an abstract reading, a faculty lecture or a contrived scenario; instead, the conversations are grounded in real experiences and events that a network member has encountered or questioned. The motivation to participate, either by passively reading the dialogue or by actively sending messages, is very high.

Year-round Education Assistance

In areas of high growth, many California schools are actively implementing year-round education in which schools operate on multiple schedules or tracks. One example of a multi-track system involves dividing the student body into four tracks. Three tracks, on a rotating basis, are always in session throughout the year. Students and teachers have class for nine weeks followed by three-week breaks. Vacation days for students and teachers are staggered so that school buildings can be cost-effective in accommodating greater numbers of students.

Some of the elements associated with year-round schools which affect beginning teacher programs are:

1) school start-ups are staggered; 2) numbers of combination classrooms (classrooms in which there are two or more grade levels) are increased to allow for every grade level to be offered on most tracks; 3) interactions between grade level teachers, advisors and new teachers, and total staff are hampered by rotating vacation schedules; and 4) "flex" teaching becomes necessary. A flex teacher is one who moves his or her students and materials into different classrooms which become available on a rotating basis through-out the school year. In some schools flexing occurs every three weeks. Veteran teachers who have first priority of assignment within most districts often avoid non-traditional assignments; therefore, a higher number of new teachers begin their teaching careers as flex teachers in combination classes on tracks that begin during the summer months.

Strategies of assistance which may be effective in traditional schools are frequently ineffective in year-round schools. Consequently, projects for assisting beginning teachers may need to implement substantially different models of assistance within the same district. Programs which currently incorporate year-round schools have suggested the following adaptations in assistance:

• Multiple training sessions covering the same content should be incorporated into the program design. For example, orientations for new teachers and initial training for advisors may need to be offered on two-to-four occasions over a time span of four months (e.g., June-September). Funds to support this duplication in training should be incorporated in the budget.

• Communications usually sent to school sites through district mail or publicized through staff bulletins must be mailed to home addresses of teachers who are off-track (on vacation). Advance program scheduling and publicity must become a high priority in order to ensure effective communication.

• Continuity of support for new teachers should be maintained, despite difficulties posed when new and experienced grade-level partners are on different tracks. Since administrators seek to offer each grade level on every track, it is common for a new teacher to be on a different track from the other grade-level teachers at the site. Thus, there are three-week periods of time scattered through-out the year when either the new teacher or the advisor is off-track. One project has approached the problem of continuity of assistance in year-round schools by establishing a support team of assisting teachers. When a new teacher's partner is off-track, the team members take over the assisting role.

- Special assistance in learning how to manage two grade-level curricula should be provided. Due to the need to provide each grade level on every track, combination classrooms are more prevalent in year-round schools. New teachers often receive these assignments. Deciding what content must be taught separately to each grade within the classroom and what content can be taught to the whole group is complex even for an experienced teacher. Consider the fact that a child enrolled as a third grader in a 3/4 combination one year, a fourth grader in a straight fourth grade the next year, and fifth grader in a 4/5 combination the following year may receive three years of content usually reserved for fourth grade when whole group instruction is the dominant instructional methodology. Yet, preparing and presenting two completely distinct lessons for five or six subject areas each day is unmanageable (particularly for the new teacher). Selection of curriculum, instructional methodology, and the coordination of instruction for specific combinations of classrooms demands uniquely different approaches from those appropriate for regular classroom instruction. District level curriculum specialists and school site resource teachers can offer focused inservice assistance to address these specific concerns.

- New teacher projects should be particularly sensitive to the needs of the "flex" teacher, the teacher who must pack up materials and students and change classrooms as they become available on a rotating schedule. One strategy advocates that the flex teacher be freed from other assignments such as playground or lunch duty. Incentives of this nature may encourage veteran teachers to accept the flex assignment or provide needed stress reduction for the new teacher.

Year-round schedules can have some benefits to new teacher programs. Experienced teachers who are off-track may be more amenable to observing and advising novice teachers when they do not need to take time away from their own classrooms to offer assistance. Frequently, however, off-track advisors are either out of town or working as substitutes, so structuring this type of support can be difficult. New teachers who are off-track can use the time to observe effective role models in classrooms that are in session. In their own buildings, this can be facilitated by project personnel and/or principals. A new teacher on a traditional schedule (September-June) could elect to spend the beginning week of school with a veteran teacher at a year-round school that starts in July or August. It should be noted that teachers can neither be required nor coerced to use vacation time to engage in school activities. Off-track assistance must be voluntary but it can be structured in ways that will be highly beneficial.

Assistance in Multicultural School Settings

California's changing demographics have created a rich diversity within its student population largely due to immigration. It has been estimated that "one in six children in the public schools statewide is an immigrant, with more than a third of a million recently arrived newcomers. In some school districts as many as 80 percent are limited- or non-English speakers. In one third of the districts in the state at least one in ten students is limited-English proficient." (Olsen,1988, p. 5.)

Despite a legal mandate to provide an equitable education for these children, there remains a significant academic gap between immigrant students and U.S.-born, English-speaking students. One critical factor in narrowing this gap is effective preservice and inservice preparation of teachers in multicultural education. Several new teacher projects have focused assistance in areas related to teaching ethnically and linguistically diverse students.

For example, the Winters School District provides new teachers with an opportunity to engage in an expense paid three-week Spanish language immersion experience in Mexico during the summer before they begin teaching. New teachers live with

Mexican host families, receive instruction relevant to their level of language proficiency, and earn university credit. The district uses this program as an incentive in hiring new teachers.

Another way to help is to offer preservice training in second language acquisition theory and approaches, alternative teaching strategies, and background on issues facing limited-English proficient students. This training should be coordinated with district-wide efforts to develop and implement English language development programs. Unfortunately, most new teachers begin teaching with minimal training in multicultural education and limited district support. Consequently, emphasis on learning to teach limited-English proficient students should be a primary focus of new teacher support and assistance programs when teachers are given assignments to teach linguistically diverse students. Two outstanding references for defining the need and the related resources are *Crossing the Schoolhouse Border: Immigrant Students and the California Public Schools* (Olsen, 1988) and *Bridges: Promising Programs for the Education of Immigrant Children* (Olsen, 1989). See the guidebook reference section, Appendix A.

Instructional bias associated with traditional competitive school structures tends to exacerbate the academic gap between white and racially diverse students. To avoid such bias, emphasis is being placed on cooperative learning structures. These structures have proven particularly effective in improving the achievement levels for African-American, Hispanic, and Native American students (Kagan, 1989). Since new teachers frequently struggle with cooperative learning, it is recommended that maximum time and intensity be devoted to theory, curriculum, methodology, and coaching when this approach to learning is selected as a content focus of new teacher support. Several California projects give university credit for semester coursework on cooperative learning. Training is offered to both new and experienced teachers so that contextual factors can be integrated into discussions and application of learning can be promoted at the school site.

Secondary Level Assistance

Although elementary and secondary new teachers have some needs in common, preliminary evaluation findings from the California New Teacher Proj-

ect have identified differences which require planning for alternative strategies of assistance. Elementary teachers have many more concerns in common with each other than with secondary teachers. Generic concerns related to school structure, classroom management, instructing the same students for the entire school day and teaching multiple subjects in the elementary program provide a common ground for interaction and assistance which is less prevalent for secondary teachers.

Secondary teachers require more narrowly focused, content-specific assistance. Although some concerns of new secondary teachers are shared across subject areas (e.g., discipline and interacting with parents), program content and strategies should emphasize curriculum concerns. Strategies of assistance should be altered to accommodate this variation of needs when a program serves both elementary and secondary teachers. One approach includes collaborative assistance — that is, district-level, subject-area coordinators and university preservice subject-area professors together providing content specific seminars using district adopted criteria and instructional materials.

It is recommended that support teams for secondary teachers be integrated into the subject area departmental structure. If all members of the department are part of the support process, the new teacher who teaches a range of grade levels or subjects within a specific discipline will have access to multiple sources of expertise. One strategy for providing the various kinds of support needed would be to allocate a specific number of release days or stipend allotments for assistance to the school site principal who could guide the department in determining appropriate structures for assistance and remuneration.

CONCLUSION

Supporting new teachers as they join the field of education is both a challenging and rewarding responsibility. Beginning teacher programs provide the bridge between preservice and inservice programs which are part of the process of developing professional educators. As Griffin (1989) states:

> We know that teaching cannot be mastered in
> a four-year dose of courses, practica, seminars,
> and student teaching. We know that what

teachers need to know, be sensitive to, and adapt for their own use must be collected, sifted, refined, and added to over a career. Learning to teach must be on-going. It must be a coherent and cumulative growth in understanding and experimentation with ideas and practices (p. 279).

There is a parallel between learning to teach and learning to assist beginning teachers. Those committed to integrating new teachers into the profession and helping them more effectively fulfill their task are — like new teachers — continually exploring and broadening their knowledge base.

REFERENCES

Evertson, C. (1989). Classroom organization and management. In M.C. Reynolds (Ed.), *Knowledge base for the beginning teacher*. New York: Pergamon Press.

Gardner, W. (1989). Preface. In M.C. Reynolds (Ed.), *Knowledge base for the beginning teacher*. New York: Pergamon Press.

Griffin, G. (1989). Coda: The knowledge-driven school. In M.C. Reynolds (Ed.), *Knowledge base for the beginning teacher*. New York: Pergamon Press.

Murphy, D.S. (1988). The impact of socialization mechanisms on the problem-solving approaches of novice teachers. (Doctoral Dissertation: The Claremont Graduate School/San Diego State University Joint Doctoral Program in Education).

Olsen, L. (1988). *Crossing the schoolhouse border: Immigrant students and the California public schools*. A California Tomorrow Policy Research Report.

Olsen, L. (1989). *Bridges: Promising programs for the education of immigrant children*.

Veenman, S. (1984). Perceived problems of beginning teachers. *Review of Educational Research*, 54(2), 143-178.

Ward, Beatrice A. (1989). Keynote Address. The California Invitational Workshop on Implementing Beginning Teacher Programs.

CHAPTER 4

The Role of Experienced Educators in Assisting New Teachers

Judith H. Shulman
Far West Laboratory for Educational Research and Development

Victoria L. Bernhardt
California State University, Chico

I am convinced that the interactions between Ms. R. and me have helped us both immensely. In helping her I found myself reflecting on my own classroom practices and striving for improvement. And she often comments about how much I have helped. In our case, the mentor-mentee relationship was beneficial. [Mentor teacher.]

I find working with Margie stimulating and rewarding. Sometimes she seems overwhelmed by the task and flounders badly. Then, in working in the group [with other new teachers] she seems to sort herself out, define the problem and use her own resources and the suggestions of others to formulate solutions. [University faculty member.]

I am having many problems juggling personal empathy, collegiality and professional help in this case. I think I became too emotionally involved from the beginning. I certainly am concerned for my ego if I am unsuccessful and Jan loses her job. [Veteran teacher.]

I feel ambivalent when I'm involved with teachers like Diane. I find myself not knowing what to say or do. [Mentor teacher.]

This chapter focuses on the educators who are assigned to help new teachers — who they are, what they do, the support they need, and the benefits and challenges of their new responsibilities. It also deals with some of the organizational arrangements that encourage or hinder the success of new teacher support programs.

We used two major sources of information to capture our knowledge of such programs. The first came from a conference in San Diego, where approximately 80 program coordinators and staff gathered to share their experiences and learn from each other. The questionnaires and group discussions from this conference are our primary sources of data. We also used data from a conference in Hayward, where representatives of Bay Area districts that either had support programs in place or were in the planning stages of developing them gathered to discuss common concerns.

The chapter begins with a description of the multitude of terms used to describe educators who assist new teachers. Next it focuses on who they are, what they do, and how they need to be supported to be effective advisors. It concludes with a discussion of common problems in the organizational arrangements of support programs, and some policy recommendations for institutions planning similar programs.

The Need for a Common Language

When we asked the 24 participants in our group discussions in San Diego what titles they gave to educators in their districts who support new teachers, they came up with twenty-one different terms. Some were different because they referred to different role groups — teachers, administrators/district staff, or university faculty. The majority however, were titles for teacher advisors. In fact, one participant listed four alternative titles, because her district could not decide what to call these teachers. Table 1 lists all of the titles within their respective role groups.

The range of titles that programs assign to teachers highlights one of the key ambiguities of new teacher support programs. How much authority comes with the role of teacher advisor? Is it a supervisory role? Or is this person a consultant who can offer suggestions? Table 1's first four titles — teacher advisor, mentor teacher, mentor emeritus, and lead teacher — appear to suggest a higher status than the remaining seven, perhaps implying more authority. The latter group appears to qualify any status differences in its titles. In our experience, most teachers who are appointed to support neophytes try to diminish such status differences. In fact, many districts that participate in the California Mentor Teacher Program[1] have changed the term "mentor teacher" to a more benign title, like "consultant teacher" or "buddy."

[1] The California Mentor Teacher Program is funded by the state's Hart-Hughes Education Reform Act of 1983 (SB 813). This legislation, in effect as of January 1, 1984, is intended to reward and retain excellent teachers and to contribute to school improvement. The statute allocates funds to participating districts on a formula basis, allowing $4000 stipends for district-designated mentors, and $2000 per mentor for district implementation. The mentors' primary role is to guide and assist new teachers; they may also guide and assist more experienced teachers and develop special curricula. The statute leaves considerable latitude for California's diverse school districts to design their own programs.

TABLE 1
TERMS FOR EDUCATORS
WHO SUPPORT NEW TEACHERS

Teachers	Administrators/District Staff
teacher advisor	principal
mentor teacher	administrator
mentor emeritus	resource teacher
lead teacher	coordinator
teacher consultant	curriculum team leader
colleague coach	site coordinator
peer coach	
peer consultant	**University**
support teacher	
teammate	help-line cadre member
help-line cadre member	university consultant
	cluster leader
	professor

Other districts use the title "peer coach" or "partner" to differentiate their advisors from other mentor teachers funded through the Mentor Teacher Program. Since the legislation states that mentor teachers may perform other functions such as staff development and curriculum development, these districts selected a term that refers specifically to assisting new teachers.

The titles used for school and district administrators denote a job title or project role and are therefore less ambiguous. The same appears true for titles of university personnel involved in the new teacher programs.

In this chapter, we will not attempt to develop a consensus on what each title means, nor on appropriate behavior norms for support teachers working with neophytes. These are issues for individual districts to decide. We have decided, however, to use the term "teacher advisor" or "advisor" to represent all of the educators, in whatever capacity, who help newcomers during their first few years of teaching.

Who Are the Advisors and What Do They Do?

Advisors wear many hats and provide a wide range of services for beginning teachers. For this discussion, we define advisors according to four role groups — veteran teachers, administrators, district staff, and university faculty. We also address some pertinent issues, such as the importance of an appro-

TABLE 2
TYPES OF ASSISTANCE OFFERED BY VETERAN TEACHERS TO NEW TEACHERS IN PROGRAMS REPRESENTED AT THE SAN DIEGO CONFERENCE

Types of Assistance	% of Programs
Observation and Coaching	50%
Obtain Resource Materials	42%
Provide Emotional Support	38%
Conduct Workshops	33%
Consultation	33%
Demonstration Lessons (e.g., curriculum management)	33%
On-site Buddy	17%
Survival Skills	13%
Introduction to School Procedures	8%
Evaluation	8%
Miscellaneous	4%
Cover Classrooms	
Teacher Advocates	
Site Coordinator for Buddies	
Attend Seminars with New Teachers	
Organize Action Research Plan	
Guest Speaker at University Seminar	

n=24

priate match between advisors and new teachers. And we describe a few programs that have unusual features.

Veteran Teachers

All of the programs use veteran teachers in a variety of capacities as advisors for new teachers. The kinds of assistance veterans can provide depend on a number of factors, such as the district's definition of the advisor role, the amount of time advisors can spend with their assigned colleagues, the number of release days the programs allot for consulting responsibilities, and the types of training, and/or support the district offers.

In the best of possible circumstances, veteran teachers can be of enormous help to beginners. They can, for example:

- Help beginners learn to meet he procedural demands of the school;

- Provide moral and emotional support and function as sounding boards for new ideas;

- Provide access to other classrooms so that novices can observe other teachers, and have several kinds of models;

- Share their own knowledge about new materials, unit planning, curriculum development, and teaching methods;

- Assist teachers with classroom management and discipline;

- Help neophytes understand the implications of student diversity for teaching and learning;

- Engage teachers in self-assessment and reflection on their own practice; and

- Help them adapt new strategies for their own classroom.

The first six types of assistance help teachers to survive in their classrooms. The last two are keys to continuous learning and increasing self-sufficiency.

One technique for promoting analysis on teaching is called *coaching* — one teacher observes another teacher conduct a lesson, makes a record that is revealing and convincing to the teacher, and then engages the teacher in an analysis of the lesson. Coaching is rewarding for the learner — if done in an environment of mutual trust. This is the aspect of mentoring that has the greatest potential for getting to the actual work of teaching.

The programs represented at the San Diego conference actively support beginning teachers (see Table 2). Half reported that veteran teachers observe and coach their beginning teachers — a very high percentage compared to most support programs (Shulman, 1987; Ruskus & Pecheone, 1989). One-third or more reported that veterans provide resource materials, emotional and moral support, individual consultation outside of class, and opportunities to watch demonstration lessons. Other activities include: 1) being an on-site buddy; 2) evaluating the performance of new teachers (see below); 3) covering new teachers' classrooms while they observe other teachers; 4) being a teacher advocate when new teachers have problems like getting supplies; 5) attending seminars with new teachers; and 6) being a guest speaker at university seminars.

California Mentor Teacher Program. Most of the programs in this sample use funding from the California Mentor Teacher Program to pay stipends to their support teachers. For some, the program represents the only source of funding available to assist new teachers. Often, mentors represent an outstanding group of teachers who have the training and expertise necessary to help newcomers.

The few programs that do not use mentor funds report specific reasons. For example, Poway Unified School District's consultants assess new teachers, which is not allowed under the mentor teacher legislation. Other programs (e.g., University of California, Riverside) use retired teachers as their teacher consultants.

Appropriate Match. The process of pairing advisors with new teachers is one of the most important keys to a successful program. Merely assigning an advisor to a new teacher is not an answer, because some relationships are not helpful. The following are some considerations that must be taken into account.

The first is *proximity* or assistance from someone at the school site. Most people seem to agree that there simply is no substitute for having someone close by when a new teacher's problems occur. However, *grade level* and *subject specialty* must also be matched. Consultants at the elementary level should have experience in or be quite knowledgeable about the particular problems of the new teacher's grade level assignment. It is especially helpful if the advisor has recently taught at the same grade level, so he or she can share materials and lesson plans.

Advisors are particularly limited when they do not understand their new teacher's content area. They cannot help their colleagues plan relevant lessons tailored to the needs of their students. Nor can they evaluate the novice's choices of instructional strategies. In these cases, advisors can only judge the appropriateness of some generic pedagogical skills. Though important, these generic skills represent only one component of the complex teaching process.

Other criteria for effective pairing are *personal chemistry* and *similar philosophies* of teaching. A match might look good on paper in terms of grade level and subject speciality compatibility. But the two individuals may have different teaching styles and beliefs. They may not even like each other.

Several programs try to solve this dilemma by providing their new teachers with more than one kind of advisor. For example, the unified school districts in Burbank, Cajon Valley, San Mateo, San Leandro, Fresno, Sacramento, and San Francisco assign both designated mentor teachers *and* site buddies to assist new teachers. The mentor teachers are usually a cadre of teachers, funded through the California Mentor Teacher Program, who may have extensive training in new teacher support. They are often subject area specialists and are trained to use coaching strategies, provide demonstration lessons, and conduct workshops. The site buddies (sometimes referred to as peer consultants, or teammates) are veteran teachers at the school site who are assigned to help newcomers with school procedures and the day-to-day problems of teaching.

Often new teachers are able to select their own site buddies. In Sacramento, San Mateo, and San Francisco unified school districts, the new teachers submit to the principal a list of teachers with whom they would like to work, and the principal makes the final decision. Usually this selection is done during the first few months of school. In all cases, the site buddies volunteer to be candidates for appointment.

Cajon Valley district has added a new dimension to this approach. Because the staff understands the importance of help during the first weeks of school, principals assign a start-up partner to each new teacher in their buildings for the first weeks of school. After the first eight weeks of the project, new teachers have input into the selection of their support team members, who are their primary consultants for the rest of the year.

Other districts use less formal measures to pair teachers, such as personal agreements between new and veteran teachers. In one case, district staff hosted a dinner for all new teachers and potential buddies. Before the dinner, the program coordinator had drafted a list of matched pairs, but before she knew it, new teachers and potential site buddies had made their own agreements. In retrospect, the coordinator felt that this pairing system probably worked better than her own scheme.

Evaluation. In California, the job of evaluating new teachers is up to site principals. They are required by law to evaluate and provide feedback to each new teacher in their building at least once a year. Two districts, however — Poway Unified School District and Santa Cruz City Schools — are piloting programs that use experienced teachers to both assist and assess the progress of new teachers during their induction year. In Poway, the experienced teachers, called "teacher consultants," are released full time to perform their designated responsibilities for a maximum of three years. Each teacher consultant has a workload of 15 new teachers and is given a $4000 stipend. Santa Cruz City Schools is piloting an adaptation of this model: principal and veteran teacher teams assist and assess new teachers together.[2] Both programs are jointly governed by the Poway and Santa Cruz Federations of Teachers respectively under a trust agreement that is renewable each year.

Administrators

Because of their time constraints and range of other responsibilities, most principals play a limited role in helping new teachers. However, conference participants agreed that active support by principals is crucial to the potential success of any support program. Some of the related functions that principals perform are: supervising teacher-coaches, assigning buddies to new teachers, providing substitutes when consultants and new teachers need release time, making referrals to consultants when teachers are in trouble, and participating in monthly meetings with new teachers and their consultants. Some participants reported that principals provide ongoing support for new teachers, but such assistance was rare.

In our experience, it is very important that both teacher advisors and building principals meet face-to-face to discuss some ground rules for their respective roles in helping new teachers. Without such ground rules, it is likely that each will have unspoken expectations for the other's responsibilities. The danger is that relationships between advisors and their new teacher-colleagues can be compromised. For example, in many districts, advisors assume that all their interactions with their colleagues are confidential.[3] Yet some mentor teachers report that they are asked by their principals to provide information on the professional growth of their colleagues. These kinds of requests put advisors in an uncomfortable position.

DISTRICT STAFF/RESOURCE TEACHERS

Several districts use district staff or resource teachers to coordinate their support program. These persons also provide substitutes, schedule district-wide events, organize workshops, and conduct advisor training. Some also work with individual advisors and new teachers.

University Faculty

Several projects involve notable collaborations between school districts and local university teacher preparation programs. The advisor roles taken by university faculty in these programs are not only different from those assumed by school persons, but they often cannot be duplicated by district personnel. Representative activities include: teaching special courses for new teachers and district advisors, conducting various seminars and workshops on the school campus, assisting with planning and curriculum development, and providing one-on-one consultation for school-based advisors and their new teachers. The next chapter describes some of the programs that are illustrative of these university-school collaboratives.

Staff Development for Advisors

Though the programs described above appear to offer a variety of support activities, staff in these programs agree that developing a constructive relationship with any new teacher is a difficult challenge. Teacher advisors often have to clear several hurdles before they are welcomed by their assigned colleagues. One of the first challenges they face is establishing a working relationship in an atmosphere of mutual trust and respect. Many new teachers are suspicious of another teacher's offer of help. Some resent such offers because they believe that they do not need any help, while others wonder if their

---

[2] *Teachers are released half-time to perform these responsibilities.*

[3] *This is often due to an interpretation of one of the regulations of the California Mentor Teacher Program which states that mentor teachers cannot evaluate other teachers.*

advisors are spies from the administration. This leaves the advisors in an awkward position. If they assert themselves too strongly, they may be perceived as rude or disruptive. If they assert themselves too little or unskillfully, they can be viewed as useless. For their error, they are likely to be rejected or ignored. The risk is that an excellent teacher could become an ineffective advisor (Bird & Little, 1985).

Another challenge for advisors, especially for mentor teachers who must demonstrate that they earn their additional stipend, is finding ways to show their colleagues that they have the expertise to be helpful. They must be able to create these opportunities, or they may find themselves all dressed up with no place to go.

Perhaps the most difficult challenge of all is coaching itself. Many teachers find it very difficult to give constructive feedback to a colleague. They ask themselves, "Who am I to mentor another teacher?" and refrain from providing appropriate guidance.

For all these reasons, new and experienced support teachers need sustained staff development in the knowledge base of teaching and the skills of advising. Yet many districts around the state appoint advisors and expect them to assert their new role without any training.

Several participants at the Hayward conference reported that this was their situation. They came to the conference because they simply had no idea where to begin. As one new advisor said, "I am the only one our of 22 mentor teachers in my district whose job is to help new teachers. What should I do?" Another participant noted, "If we start programs without taking into account that advisors may not be ready to assist because they feel insecure about their new role, we've done a disservice to our new teachers." This guidebook provides a list of resources that can be used as a starting point for planning inservice activities.

Programs represented at the San Diego conference appear to be more sophisticated in their regard for the importance of additional training for advisors. They reported offering a variety of activities to their advisors. The most frequently described workshops focus on peer coaching or clinical supervision. They range from a one-day seminar to the six-day cognitive coaching series offered by Art Costa and Robert Garmston. Other workshop topics include effective teaching, the needs of new teachers, adult learning, group facilitation and communication skills, and presentation skills.

Our questionnaires and discussions on advisor training programs brought two disturbing revelations. First, there is an apparent lack of focus on the implications of student diversity for teaching and learning. This finding was surprising, since multicultural education appears to be a dominant theme in some university seminars. This content is included in several preservice programs (see previous chapter) and in university seminars for new teachers and their advisors (see next chapter). With the growth of minority populations in California, we believe that strategies for teaching diverse student populations ought to be imbedded in the training of all advisors, so that they can help new teachers meet the needs of their students.

The second revelation is the lack of emphasis on content and subject matter issues. A few programs mentioned sending their teacher advisors and new teachers to subject-specific conferences. These kinds of conferences are definitely helpful. Yet context-specific issues must also be addressed during the generic coaching seminars that are so popular.

A Case Approach. Perhaps the most important staff development takes place during regularly scheduled meetings where teacher advisors come together to discuss common concerns and share experiences. As teachers present their own personal "cases" and receive critical feedback from their colleagues, they can begin to develop some coaching strategies that work for them. By analyzing one another's cases, the advisors can find precedents for action and can generate some principles that apply across cases.

Far West Laboratory, in collaboration with the Los Angeles Unified School District, used a combination of case writing and case presentations to develop *The Mentor Teacher Casebook* (Shulman & Colbert, 1988). This book was developed by a group of mentor teachers who met weekly in a course taught by Joel Colbert. They presented their written narratives to one another, then used the cases as a springboard for analyzing appropriate behavior. Several mentors noted that writing the narratives helped them reflect on their practices with new teachers and raised their consciousness about the dimensions of the mentor's role. Equally important, they said, was the opportunity to share experiences and concerns with their colleagues and to learn alternative ways of handling diverse situations. The mentors learned that they were not alone — that their experiences were not unique.

Far West Laboratory currently uses a similar case approach in its own mentor training workshops. Beginning with selected published cases, advisors analyze the issues in each case and share related personal experiences. These deliberations are often used as the basis for developing a set of district norms that advisors can subsequently use with their new teachers.

BENEFITS/INCENTIVES

If the advisor's job is at times ambiguous and demanding, what are its benefits? What incentives do projects use to encourage teachers to apply?

Personal growth and satisfaction are the biggest pluses according to most participants. As one put it, "There is a stipend for mentor teachers, but the largest benefit is renewal — an increased vigor and enthusiasm for teaching." Others told of satisfaction from helping the new teacher survive the first and second year experience, from ensuring that their own novice trauma was not suffered by someone else, or from sharing years of experience with others. "I can now repay those educators who helped me through the years," said one consultant.

Still others said they benefitted from increased reflection on their own teaching; release time to get additional training and go to conferences; an increased sense of professionalism; recognition in the district; an increase in self-esteem; friendship; and stipends or mini-grants to buy supplies.

Incentives. Increased remuneration and release time are the most highly touted incentives to applying for an advisor position. The remuneration in this sample ranges from the mentor stipend of $4000 to consultant fees of $50 per teacher. One program gives $15 per hour for consulting; another, funded by a private foundation, offers each consultant a $150 mini-grant to buy supplies. Other incentives include: extended professional development opportunities, reduced fees for university courses, university credits which move them up the salary scale, certificates

and letters of appreciation from the central office, and autonomy over the mentor administrative budget. University faculty and district level personnel most frequently participated as part of their regular work load and as such did not receive extra remuneration.

One participant at the Hayward conference mourned her high school district's lack of a support program for new teachers. Since the district used the California Mentor Teacher Program funds for teachers who had interesting projects, no money remained to provide financial incentives for advisors. A committee is developing a support program, but as they try to find teachers to participate, the typical response is, "New teachers should suffer like I did during my first year."

FACTORS THAT CAN IMPEDE SUCCESS

We have seen that appropriate matching of new teachers and advisors, inservice training, benefits and incentives can be keys to the success of new teacher support programs. Next we turn to some of the factors that can impede success. The first is selection procedures because they are often the most controversial part of a support program.

Selection and Renominating Procedures. There is probably no more important predictor of program success than the perceived quality of the teachers selected as advisors. Unless the new teachers believe that the advisors are worthy of their appointments and are credible in their role, they will not request assistance. As one new teacher told us:

> My mentor teacher came to see me yesterday and asked if I had any problems. I responded that I needed help with my ninth grade English class, and proceeded to describe what I was currently doing. He gave me some advice, like going to the curriculum library and changing seat assignments, all of which I had already done. At the end of our conference, it was clear that I had already pursued all of his suggestions. That was the last time I saw my mentor. He teaches advanced English classes and clearly knew nothing about the problems of ninth grade English.

Our discussion of selection procedures is divided into two parts: the selection of site buddies and the selection of mentor teachers. Most of the programs use a process similar to one of these. An examination of renominating procedures concludes this section.

Selecting Site Buddies. As described earlier in this chapter, several projects provide a site buddy for each new teacher, i.e., an experienced teacher who volunteers to help a new teacher in his or her building. In most districts, site principals make these selections. They try to find teachers who are themselves successful, are committed to the notion of new teacher support, and are matched according to subject and/or grade level. Most principals pair site buddies with new teachers with the consent of the veterans themselves. In some districts, new teachers consult on the selection of their own buddies. In others, the collaborating universities select the buddies. Often they select teachers who have already gone through their own cooperating teacher training.

Selecting Mentor Teachers. A mentor teacher is one who is funded by the California Mentor Teacher Program. The state legislation contains certain restrictions on the program:

1) Mentor teachers must be credentialed, classroom teachers with permanent status.

2) The selection committee for mentor teachers must be made up of a majority of teachers.

3) Mentor teachers can serve for up to three years, with an opportunity to reapply.

The selection procedures for mentor teachers are potentially quite controversial because of the accompanying stipend and other benefits for each mentorship. In general, the projects report positive receptions to their selection criteria. Some mentors and other teachers, however, said that political factors influenced selections.

In most districts, selections are based on a combination of application screening and interviews. Some programs add classroom observations, in an attempt to ensure excellence. But without painstaking care, the observation process can backfire. The observation instrument must be perceived as valid, which itself is difficult, and in order for observers to use the instrument appropriately, they need extensive training that is often too time-consuming for districts to undertake.

Moreover, educational researchers and scholars are becoming increasingly convinced of the limitations of one or two brief observations (e.g., Stodolsky, 1988), which is all that most districts have time to conduct. They assert that to establish "typical teaching performance," many more classroom visits are needed than have ever been used for evaluation (L. Shulman, 1988; Stodolsky, 1988). As Lee Shulman said in an interview for this chapter, "The most we can say from one or two brief observations is that the teachers observed will not be a complete disaster."

One problem is that no existing evaluation procedures for judging excellence are generally perceived as valid by the teaching profession. Districts must convince teachers that their evaluation system is legitimate and not capricious. At the very least, teachers should be entitled to see the evaluation instrument on which they are judged. We know of at least one urban district that does not allow its teachers access to their own observation instrument. We believe this to be an untenable position.

Renomination. Renomination refers to advisors whose term is ending (e.g., those funded through the Mentor Teacher Program have a limited term with an opportunity to reapply). Ideally, renomination is based on a viable monitoring system that reflects the way in which advisors work together with their colleagues. Unfortunately, this is rarely the case. One of the most common questions we are asked is how to evaluate advisors. Most districts use a combination of mentor logs and principal recommendations, neither of which is usually valid. Mentor logs are infrequently monitored. And principals are not usually privy to the quality of interactions between advisors and their colleagues.

One alternative, which appears to be in the formative stages in some projects around the country, is the development of a portfolio that documents the kinds of activities that advisors and their colleagues do together. Sample entries that advisors could include are: action plans worked on together, documented observations and conferences, and feedback forms or recommendations from colleague teachers. This portfolio could be used as one source of data on which candidates are examined during the renomination process.

PROBLEMS/CONSTRAINTS AND POSSIBLE SOLUTIONS

For the most part, California teachers appear enthusiastic about beginning teacher support programs. Conference participants, however, noted several problems that constrained their programs' success. This section will describe some of these problems and potential solutions that have been developed.

Time. Lack of time to work together was the most frequently noted constraint. "There is so much to do, and so little time to do it," reported several participants. Moreover, some advisors have so many requests from new teachers, that they feel overwhelmed. Others complain about the time it takes to visit new teachers at different school sites. Their solution is to consult only by telephone.

Since time during school is at a premium, many advisors meet with their new teachers after school or during lunch. Others arrange a common prep period to consult. The disadvantage of these options is that teachers have less time to themselves, their students, and their families.

Release Time/Substitutes. Even if advisors have release time available, most hesitate to use it. Their major reason is the general lack of good substitutes. These teachers care deeply about the quality of instruction their students receive, and they hesitate to submit their students to poor teaching. One advisor at the conference said, "I can't rely on subs to teach according to my lesson plans, so I gave a test today." Another said, "I showed a movie." Teacher consultants in Connecticut's Beginning Educator Training and Support Program (BEST) reported similar reasons for not using their allocated release time to work with their beginning teachers (Ruskus & Pecheone, 1989).

Advisors also hesitate to provide release time for their new teachers to visit other veterans. Though they agree that these visits are usually beneficial, particularly when they can go together and debrief the observation, they are reluctant to submit their teachers to potential chaos upon returning to their classrooms.

Individually, conference participants were hard-pressed to come up with viable solutions to these problems. One program coordinator described good results with permanent substitutes who were hired specifically for advisor activities. Several conference participants thought that permanent substitutes could be a viable option for their programs.

As a group, participants brainstormed some other alternatives. Everyone agreed that an effective support program cannot depend on the availability of good substitutes, because they are becoming increasingly scarce as more permanent teaching positions open up. One possibility is to change the organizational framework of the system. For example, at the secondary level, advisors could team-teach groups of children. At specified times during the day, one teacher could take over the entire group, while the other would be free to consult with teachers. Another alternative is to hire recently retired teachers as advisors. Several programs in California are already using retirees, with excellent results. They have more time to devote to new teachers than do regular classroom teachers, and are enthusiastic about their new role.

A third option is to assign certain teachers full-time consulting responsibilities for no more than three years (as in Poway Unified School District). A surprising number of conference participants preferred this option to their current state of despair over being torn in several directions.

Administrative Support. While many participants praised the support they receive from their principals, others feel that their principals sabotage their programs. For example, one stated that her principal refuses to allow mentors to use release time, even though they are entitled to it through the California Mentor Teacher Program. Others said that their principals disapprove of any absence from the school site. One plan to counter such resistance is to ensure that administrators are included in the planning and staff development of new teacher support programs. Some districts have thought very carefully about the need to support veteran teachers as they assume advisor responsibilities, but have neglected to put equal thought into helping principals deal constructively with teachers' new roles as instructional leaders. One strategy is to have meetings of administrator and advisor teams, so they can develop some agreements for working together. At the very least, district staff and advisors should keep their principals informed of support activities.

Year-round Education. Organizing support programs for neophytes who teach in year-round schools offers several unique challenges. One advantage is the availability of off-track teachers as substitutes. This both enhances the pool of qualified substitutes and provides teachers with an opportunity to make more money. A disadvantage is the complexity of planning the program. Scheduling workshops and matching advisors with new teachers is often a nightmare because of multiple track schedules.

District Hiring Procedures. Several advisors noted the difficulty of achieving an effective support program when teachers are hired at the last minute or, as in some cases, well into the school year. The teachers rarely get the kind of support they need, because of the lack of time and personnel to plan accordingly. The solution appears simple. Hire new faculty early enough so that both they and their advisors have the necessary time to plan for the new year.

Inappropriately Matched Pairs. What should happen when it is clear that some new teachers are not working well with their assigned consultants? This is a common and delicate question. The most common advice is to be flexible and try to change assignments. Often it is helpful if at least one person in the project is given the responsibility to solve such problems. That person should be available to both advisors and new teachers, and should be adept at mediating difficulties.

Sometimes it is not possible to find appropriate matches in content areas and grade levels at a building site, but it is possible to pair teachers who share common beliefs about teaching and work well together. In these cases, advisors should broker relationships with other veteran teachers who are more substantively qualified.

Unclear Role Definition. Many advisors complained that they were unclear about what was expected of them. Districts must deal with these difficult questions of role expectations, or there will be rhetoric about new teacher support without much substance.

Perhaps the appropriate place to deal with such issues is during advisor meetings, where advisors can work out, over time, a consensus of appropriate norms of interaction. Districts with only one or two teacher consultants should provide time for advisors from neighboring communities to meet together. County offices and local universities are often good places to host such meetings.

RECOMMENDATIONS

In this chapter we described who the advisors are, what they do, the support they need, and the benefits and challenges of their new responsibilities. We also analyzed selected problems and constraints of the organizational arrangements that either encourage or hinder the effectiveness of their work. Finally, we offered potential solutions to some of these problems. Based on all of this information, we have created a list of recommendations for institutions to consider when planning their own support for beginning teacher programs.

- Provide training in the skills of coaching and the knowledge base of teaching for all advisors. Demonstrated excellence in teaching children does not automatically lead to excellence in advising other teachers.

- Define expectations for advisor roles, and then provide ongoing opportunities for advisors to collaboratively develop norms for appropriate interaction.

- Provide time for advisors and new teachers to work together during the school day.

- Limit the case load for each advisor to a reasonable number of new teachers.

- Make teacher support a routine part of district business so that teachers will develop the expectation that they should collaborate and learn from one another.

- Ensure that the selection procedures are acceptable to a majority of teachers.

- Select advisors who are credible, well-matched, and committed to assisting new teachers.

- Develop a monitoring system that reflects and documents the ways that advisors and new teachers work together.

- Enlist the support of administrators in the planning and implementation of the assistance program.

- Be creative in organizing arrangements that encourage constructive support for new teachers.

If these principles can be followed, more new teachers will echo the sentiments voiced by this young novice:

> "I could not have lasted had it not been for my mentor. Thank God for the mentor program!"

REFERENCES

Bird, T., & Little, J.W. (1985). *From teacher to leader: Training and support for instructional leadership by teachers.* San Francisco: Far West Laboratory for Educational Research and Development.

Ruskus, J. A., & Pecheone, R. (1989). *Making mentoring matter.* Paper presented at the annual meeting of the American Educational Research Association, San Francisco.

Shulman, J.H., & Colbert J.A. (Eds.). (1985). *The mentor teacher casebook.* San Francisco: Far West Laboratory for Educational Research and Development; and Eugene, OR: ERIC Clearinghouse on Educational Management.

Shulman, L.S. (1988). A union of insufficiencies: Strategies for teacher assessment in a period of educational reform. *Educational Leadership,* 46(3), 36-41.

Stodolsky, S. (1988). *The subject matters.* Chicago: University of Chicago Press.

CHAPTER 5

The Role of the University in New Teacher Programs

Victoria L. Bernhardt
California State University, Chico

Judith H. Shulman
Far West Laboratory for Educational Research and Development

T HE current crisis in education and impending teacher shortages argue persuasively for alterations in current teacher education practices at all levels. Traditional formulas of classroom "theory and practice" lectures, supervised student teaching, and first year trial-and-error survival tactics are not guaranteed to produce adequate, let alone excellent, instructional leaders for today's students. Increasingly, universities and school districts are recognizing that in order to prepare teachers effectively, there is a need for continuous and relevant instruction starting with the undergraduate program and extending into the professional development years.

This new thinking about teacher preparation is reflected in university delivery of on-site beginning teacher support and professional development. These programs are designed to help new teachers make the difficult transition from student teacher to professional teacher — aiding these new professionals in the integration of content knowledge, instructional theories and strategies, and interpersonal skills that they have learned in the university setting. Through involvement in new teacher programs, universities are developing new and expanded definitions of their role in teacher preparation. They are also working in partnership with practitioners to devise "extended curricula for professional teaching" that make sense. So the university's increased understanding of the products of its programs and increased awareness of typical novice teaching conditions are leading to better teacher preparation programs.

Beginning teacher programs are being established to improve the effectiveness of new teachers, increase the retention rates of capable new teachers, promote professionalism, and build commitment to professional development and life-long learning. University faculty can perform many of the roles that are a part of achieving these goals, ranging from design of the program to delivery of instructional and psychological support to supervision and coaching of the beginning teachers. Many of these roles can also be carried out by experienced teachers and administrators working in the field. In some instances, each plays a different and crucial part.

These collaborations have been documented as having a positive impact on new teacher development. Benefits to the participating university and school district are also apparent. The university's ability to see the performance of its graduates becomes crucial to enhancing its preservice training programs. As one university beginning teacher project director said:

> Our collaboration with the [school district] has helped our faculty learn about and deal with the real world of the classroom. By extending our involvement with teacher preparation into the teacher's first year, we can help new teachers apply what they have learned at the university to the real world setting.

A university faculty member reports:

Advising new teachers has given me the opportunity to participate in problem-solving in a way that has been professionally stimulating and rewarding. I deeply value confronting the realities of the initial year of teaching and 'walking through the minds of new teachers, as we collaboratively analyze alternative possibilities. Through our interactions, I feel that I have gained insight on how to more effectively prepare student teachers for the challenges they will encounter.

Districts also profit from their involvement with the university. One district project collaborator said:

> Working with the university has been great this year. They were able to do some things we could not do from the district base. The university offered graduate level units as an incentive for teachers to participate, and they assisted our teachers in establishing their professional growth plans. The university received extremely high ratings on the small group support network that they operated for beginning teachers during the year. The university was able to operate the group on a fully trusting, confidential basis.

A university faculty member adds:

> They have things we don't have and we have things they don't have. By working together and sharing our resources we both benefitted greatly — not only now, but in the future. Working together on this project has led to collaboration on other projects and increased coordination between preservice and inservice.

Clearly a new partnership in the effective preparation, long-term retention, and enhanced professionalism of teachers is emerging among schools, districts, and universities through their joint execution of beginning teacher projects.

Advantages of University Leadership in New Teacher Programs

One traditional function of colleges of education has been the advancement of knowledge and the dissemination of research findings to practitioners in the field. As part of their university role, education faculty engage in basic and applied research and other forms of scholarship. They communicate their new knowledge through teaching, publications, presentations, and consultations. In their professional field, education faculty have a special responsibility to guide the integration of new knowledge with practice, including consultations with public school personnel, and the development, piloting, and evaluation of new teaching models.

Traditionally, university faculty have disseminated new knowledge by teaching at the preservice level and providing inservice to school personnel. New education studies, however, show that beginning teachers have a crucial need for specific kinds of information, as well as for guidance and nurturing in professional skill-building as they assume responsibility for their own classrooms. Further, the studies show that in the absence of this information and professional leadership, large numbers of gifted teachers leave the profession at the end of their first year of teaching. Universities have a unique capability to develop comprehensive and intensive programs around both state-of-the-art knowledge and local priorities. Working collaboratively with local schools, they can both support beginning teachers and create career ladders for experienced teachers in ways that are designed to develop autonomous educational professionals.

> [By collaborating with a university in the support of new teachers] the district sees an opportunity in capitalizing on the strengths of new teachers. Universities are capable of contributing the research base and theoretical knowledge of teaching, while school districts bring the practical, craft knowledge of teaching to the support process. (District project director)

> Before we began our collaboration with [the university], we had a traditional view of how to support beginning teachers. Our staff development activities focused on providing prescriptions and/or strategies that would enable teachers to survive teaching. That focus has now changed. Our interactions with university faculty have forced us to move beyond this survival mode to one of developing reflective practitioners who are able to analyze their own teaching and make thoughtful decisions.... Rather than mandate standards and prescribe how to achieve those standards as the Board and administration have done in the past, we

> want to involve teachers in setting the standards and determining how to achieve them. (District project director)

An abundance of content area experts and other resources can be found at universities and brought to the beginning teacher as needs arise. University-based specialists in such diverse fields as multicultural education, English as a second language, educational measurement, biology, mathematics, or geography, can be recruited to meet specific beginning teacher needs. Further, expanded access to university resources such as curriculum libraries, computer hardware and software laboratories, and curriculum and instructional consultants can enhance the growth of teachers during their early years in the profession, guiding them into sound educational practice.

Teacher preparation faculty can provide "safe" instruction to new teachers as they attempt to sort out the problems and conditions of their new profession and working environment. The supervisory and evaluative relationships teachers previously formed with university personnel can be extended into coaching and advising relationships during the beginning teacher's first years. Because this enhanced relationship is external to employer/employee personnel processes, it is confidential, non-evaluative, and advisory. Continuing interaction can be focused on meeting the perceived needs of beginning teachers when and where they need it — in the classroom. Instruction is driven by the beginning teacher's "itch to know" and desire to provide the best possible learning situation for students, apart from questions of evaluation and professional survival.

Additionally, universities offer valuable incentives for participation in proven beginning teacher programs. Graduate units, enabling teachers to move up on district salary schedules, are awarded. Networks for sharing ideas and reducing professional isolation are created. Access to centralized resource banks and content specialists is granted in a format that encourages teachers to make use of them. The opportunity to participate in professional development activities is guaranteed even to the most geographically isolated teachers, keeping them up-to-date with the latest developments in the field. Perhaps most important, a link to career-long and life-long learning is established early in each teacher's professional life.

Universities can also assure continuity and broad dissemination of knowledge gained from new teacher programs. At instructional seminars or workshops they can reach teachers from many school districts at once. Often such seminars are the only access small school districts have to needed professional development activities. By bringing teachers from many schools together, universities can help establish a network that teachers can then use to share ideas and reduce the isolation inherent to the profession.

Many universities also have technological capabilities that allow them to interface with teachers over great distances. Such capabilities include instructional television (California State University, Chico), electronic bulletin boards (University of California, Riverside), and toll-free telephone hot lines (California State University, Northridge) — facilities too expensive for all but the largest districts to finance and fully utilize. One school board president reinforces this point:

> We're in an isolated mountain community. Without the university, our staff would have no opportunities for comprehensive professional development. The university included us in the development of the beginning teacher program and then brought it to us! They also helped us support each other through a structure and training that we couldn't, and probably wouldn't have, established on our own. Most of all, by including us with other teachers from many other communities, they helped lessen our feelings of isolation and deprivation. We now have a large network of teachers and university faculty to draw from.

Such enthusiastic reactions are typical of school districts, both urban and rural, working jointly with universities to find cutting edge solutions that work.

In some cases, university faculty can provide services to new teachers when public school teachers and staff are unable to do so. School personnel, for example, are often too busy initiating their own classes to assist new teachers during the critical first few weeks of school. Some school districts do not select their mentor teachers until after school starts. Thus, university faculty are frequently the only personnel available to actually coach new teachers in these early weeks.

Finally, universities are important resource partners, particularly in developing a centralized bank of information and skilled personnel that can be tapped quickly to help novices. Beginning teacher programs must meet the needs of participants in a timely way if they are to merit funding the dedication of financial and human resources in tight budget times. Through formative and summative evaluations, program content and timing must be continually revised and refined to coincide as closely as possible with the optimal moment for new teacher's learning. This implies the construction and maintenance of a data bank sophisticated enough to suit diverse content and geographic needs — clearly a job best handled jointly by university personnel, experienced teachers, administrators, and beginning teachers.

The need for formative and summative evaluation of new approaches to teacher preparation cannot be overstated. Accountability of local schools and districts as well as teacher preparation institutions must be above reproach if their efforts are to be fully supported by public dollars. The excellence of public education is closely tied to the availability of excellent teachers and excellent teacher preparation programs. Teacher preparation programs must provide clear evidence that they are effective in preparing personnel to meet the demands of the modern classroom. Summative evaluation is key to the designation of programs and program components that effectively and reliably meet the needs of teachers and students, and that merit institutionalization by teacher preparation institutions.

EXAMPLES OF UNIVERSITIES TAKING THE LEAD IN BEGINNING TEACHER PROGRAMS

The Induction for the Beginning Teacher Program based at California State University, Chico was developed in collaboration with teachers and administrators from the 14 counties in the 36,000 square mile service area of rural Northern California. The program provides all schools in the area with the opportunity to participate in professional development, and in part comes to the school via live, interactive instructional television. The program is structured to provide two sources of help for beginning teachers: 1) day-to-day support and assistance from on-site, experienced teachers, and 2) comprehensive and well-researched programming and action planning from the university for their continuing education.

A consortium of 21 school districts formed by the Riverside and San Bernardino County Offices of Education is offering five models of new teacher support through the University of California, Riverside. These programs include a telecommunications network, curriculum workshops, extended university supervision, peer coaching, and mentor teacher support. A comparative analysis of the five models will be conducted by the consortium to determine the most effective approaches for the districts involved.

The Los Angeles Unified School District has targeted four inner-city junior high schools that have high student drop-out and teacher turn-over rates for assistance through California State University, Dominguez Hills. Support teams consisting of two to four new teachers and an experienced coach or mentor teacher have been formed. New teachers are enrolled in special classroom management and cooperative learning courses taught by university faculty who are familiar with these teachers' classroom challenges. The project is experimenting with school-level cooperative learning as an approach to teacher development as well as the use of cooperative learning strategies in the classroom.

These examples illustrate the many settings in which innovative district/university partnerships operate and the diverse roles participants play in the training, long-term retention, and professional development of beginning teachers.

Summary

Teacher preparation is increasingly viewed as a process that extends into the first few years of teaching and involves university and school personnel in collaborative arrangements. Each partner can make unique as well as similar contributions to the development of teachers. A variety of collaborative arrangements exist to accommodate the diversity of needs and settings of new teachers, districts, and universities. Program strengths generated by university involvement include:

- training that is comprehensive, research based, and customized to local needs and priorities;

- enhanced access to university resources, including human resources, libraries, computer laboratories, and research support systems;

- research knowledge to inform school activities and programs and to evaluate new teacher programs;

- extensive expertise in subject matter fields and in areas of special relevance to education, e.g. multicultural education, linguistics, and educational technology;

- cost-effective delivery of programs across district boundaries resulting in multiplied effects of teacher networking;

- cost-effective delivery of programs throughout widely dispersed geographic areas creating classrooms without walls for many teachers who might not be able to participate in other forms of professional development;

- establishment of "third party" structures which promote continuous new teacher learning in "safe" environments — apart from legal requirements — for supervision and evaluation of new teachers; and

- improved dissemination of information throughout the education community.

The needs of beginning teachers are not fundamentally different from the needs of other new professionals — integration of theory and practice in the context of the working environment is key to their success. In collaboration with practitioners in the schools, the university can be a strong force in helping develop, deliver, and evaluate new teacher programs.

CHAPTER 6

Program Administration

Louise Bay Waters
California State University, Hayward

Carolyn Cates
Far West Laboratory

Cynthia Harris
Oakland Unified School District

THREE questions drive the design of an effective new teacher support project. First, *what are the goals of the project?* Typically, these include providing psychological support and orientation to beginning teachers, helping them acquire specific instructional methodologies, reducing their isolation, increasing their ability to teach children from diverse cultures and languages, helping them become better problem-solvers, and evaluating them for retention decisions. The second important question is *what personnel, programs, organizations, and other resources are necessary to achieve these goals?* And third, how can these resources be mobilized, *how can support for the project be generated?* This chapter addresses the latter two questions, with some additional comments about collaboration, a critical ingredient in all projects that cross departmental and organizational boundaries.

POTENTIAL ADMINISTRATIVE RESOURCES

Many new teacher projects in California, whether grant funded or not, are built around the school district's staff development office and mentor programs. Additionally, projects frequently involve the school district's personnel department and a teachers' association. If outside funding is available, a nearby university is sometimes involved or, less frequently, the county office of education. Each of these potential participants brings its own perspectives and resources to the support of beginning teachers. However, each must make certain changes in its traditional practices in order to contribute fully to the assistance of new teachers.

District Staff Development Offices

In most large districts, the staff development office provides programs for the instructional support of teachers, including the state's Mentor Teacher Program. These programs make staff development the logical home for beginning teacher support programs, since training is already offered on topics useful to new teachers, such as cooperative learning and classroom management. Moreover, staff development offices are typically the site of resource personnel, inservices, professional development opportunities, teacher resource centers and instructional materials collections. They commonly offer training in peer coaching which also indirectly benefits new teachers by supporting partner teachers.

On a process level, principals in most large districts already turn to the staff development office to provide curricular and instructional support to teachers in need. Collaborating with the staff development office to meet the needs of new teachers is a logical extension of this relationship. Traditionally, the director of the staff development office also holds a cabinet-level position in the district. This ready access to top-level decision makers can be important to the success of a new teacher project.

Since districts have only recently begun to hire significant numbers of new teachers, most staff development programs have not yet differentiated their services for new and veteran teachers. This differentiation is an important step in designing a new teacher program. Staff development programs must focus their efforts to support new teachers at the beginning of the year at their school sites or on a one-to-one basis, as well as in district-wide workshops.

Mentor Programs

The role of the California Mentor Teacher Program in new teacher projects is substantial. For districts that receive no internal or external funding for new teacher support, the mentor program may be the only existing vehicle to assist new teachers. In some districts, one or a small cadre of mentor teachers use their mentor time to help manage the support program. According to the New Haven New Teacher Project and the San Mateo City Project U.S., there is an advantage to having mentors fill this role: new teachers seem to be more willing to express their concerns and frustrations to the mentor serving as program manager than to district administrators in the same role.

Along with project management, mentors typically provide workshops, beginning-of-the-year orientation, or one-on-one assistance. In the Oakland-California State University Hayward New Teacher Support Project, mentors provide individualized assistance from the day new teachers are hired until late October and are on call the rest of the year for special problems. This strategy provides critical initial support while allowing the project enough time to locate and match teachers with their on-site partners.

In many districts, the existing mentor program had to be restructured to allow for maximum interaction between mentors and new teachers. For example, mentors are frequently selected on the basis of project proposals — usually curricular in nature — rather than on their interest or ability to work with new teachers. Both Winters and Upland school districts have changed their selection procedures to choose mentors who are specifically interested in helping new teachers. To facilitate partnerships between mentors and new teachers, many districts have found it valuable to provide release time to mentors to observe and model instructional techniques in new teachers' classrooms. Districts that do not participate in the Mentor Teacher Program must identify other ways to offer the teacher-to-teacher support that mentors can provide.

District Personnel Offices

Close coordination between new teacher support programs and the personnel office is critical to the success of such programs. It is the personnel office that initially interacts with new teachers and can facilitate prompt identification and referral to new teacher services. On a more fundamental level, the personnel office — in response to higher district decisions —

determines when new teachers will be hired. If the personnel office hires new teachers either at the last minute or after the school year begins, a new teacher support program does not have enough time to provide adequate initial assistance.

Because personnel practices are important to the success of new teachers, the personnel office is the administrative home for some new teacher projects. Whether it carries primary responsibility for the project or is merely closely affiliated with it, some districts need to make changes in their traditional personnel practices. First, the personnel office must develop a mechanism to identify new hires as opposed to rehires on temporary contract. Second, it must differentiate between teachers who are new to teaching and those who are simply new to the district or new to a particular school or subject area. Third, they and top district administrators must be aware of the need to try to place new teachers long before the beginning of the school year.

Teachers' Associations

A teachers' association can be a valuable player in the success of a beginning teacher project. Because of the vulnerability of new teachers in terms of assignments, lay-offs, and tenure, teachers' associations are generally well aware of the novice's special needs. In addition, both the National Education Association and the American Federation of Teachers have established national programs to encourage local affiliates to provide support to new teachers.

The relationship between certain elements of new teacher programs and bargaining issues can make the involvement of teachers' associations critical. To begin with, the design and restrictions placed on the Mentor Program are the result of collective bargaining. Similarly, project benefits such as stipends and release time for either new teachers or their partner teachers can touch on contractual agreements. Projects that wish to be closely tied to either new teacher assessment or to the development of induction schools need to work closely with an association in both the design and implementation phases.

The project most heavily involved in teacher assessment in California, the Poway New Teacher Project, is directly administered by the local teachers' association. In Poway, the program manager is a key association member. Both support and assessment are carried out by a committee of association representatives and district administrators. This committee directs individualized support during the year and makes ultimate retention decisions in the spring.

Universities

A number of grant-funded new teacher projects have strong university involvement, while others include the university in an advisory role. In the latter type of project, the university advisor primarily serves as a link to university courses and resources. In the former, university participation can occur in a variety of ways.

The most common form of close university involvement is the development of special university courses for new teachers, partner teachers or both. In the Chico Induction for Beginning Teachers Program, courses for both partners and new teachers are delivered to widely separated consortium districts via the university's instructional television station (see Chapter 5). In addition, a university staff member might serve as the primary director in a consortium of districts, or as the co-director of a collaborative project with a specific district.

University involvement in leadership is advantageous because it is easier to release a university professor than to buy out a district administrator's time. This time factor, along with the different nature of the two jobs, can allow university personnel to develop a more concentrated focus on the project than many district administrators are able to have. That focus can be particularly helpful during a project's start-up phase.

University participants also generally have greater access to literature and research on teacher induction and on programs in other districts. In addition, the university can provide evaluation services, since district evaluators are frequently overburdened with student testing and report compilation. Such ongoing evaluation has played a central role in the Riverside County/San Bernardino County New Teacher Project. Their five different new teacher support projects are being provided through five districts and two county offices. Personnel from the University of California at Riverside function as key members of the management team with the responsibility to continually assess the five models and provide feedback on them. University involvement in management can also provide administrative flexibility in such areas as travel, purchase of materials and use of rooms.

The last form of university participation is direct, one-on-one consultation with beginning teachers. Such involvement is difficult in districts serving large numbers of beginning teachers, but it offers benefits to smaller programs. Professors have the flexibility to observe and coach on a weekly or biweekly basis — something that mentor teachers with their own classrooms find it difficult to do.

University observers/coaches are also generally acquainted with a range of observation sites and instructional resources outside of the district, knowledge that is potentially valuable to new teachers. Professors outside the university teacher preparation departments are one such resource, particularly for secondary teachers. In the Oakland-CSU Hayward New Teacher Support Project, physics and biology faculty have provided supplies, lent and repaired equipment for science teachers, and helped new teachers set up demonstrations.

As with each of the other potential contributors discussed above, universities must make certain changes in traditional perspectives and practices in order to contribute effectively to induction efforts. First, universities must see that their responsibility for teacher preparation extends beyond granting teaching credentials. Second, professors must become aware of the realities of the typical first-year teacher's classroom. Normally, student teachers are placed in the best classrooms with the best master teachers who have located or purchased the best materials. This is not the usual classroom situation encountered by new teachers. Third, university leaders must be aware that new teachers have a survival orientation and have difficulty absorbing much beyond the immediately applicable. Finally, teacher preparation programs do not usually participate with districts in projects involving shared leadership. Collaboration is a process that has to be learned by members of these programs.

While each of these changes is critical to successful university involvement in new teacher support, each also contributes to improved preservice teacher education. The more professors are aware of the needs of beginning teachers, the more realistic and useful credential programs will be. Similarly, university-district collaboration that assists beginning teachers will encourage more collaboration in other teacher education programs. For example, one spin-off of the Oakland-CSU Hayward New Teacher Support Project is the new collaborative Urban Intern Program for credential candidates interested in inner-city education.

County Offices of Education

A county office of education plays a major role in only two of the state-funded new teacher projects. However, in smaller, non-funded projects, county offices can provide substantial services to an informal group of districts. Such services typically include courses or support groups for beginning teachers or their partner teachers. They also provide an opportunity for participating districts to form networks and share ideas. For example, the Alameda County Office of Education sponsored a New Teacher Recognition dinner and afternoon conference for all beginning teachers in the county who were completing their first year. At this writing, county offices of education are an under-utilized source of support for beginning teacher programs, but they are a source that will probably grow in importance as more districts sponsor their own programs.

GENERATING SUPPORT

As outlined above, there are many potential contributors to new teacher programs. However, contributions are not automatic. They must be sought, and support must be cultivated. Three of the most successful ways of generating support include collaborative planning, building from the success of existing programs, and providing a valued service. The more effectively potential participants are involved in the initial planning or grant writing, the more they feel a sense of ownership. Once initial plans have been made, continued input via an advisory committee and regular communication can maintain this commitment. Project reports can be scheduled regularly on principals' and the superintendent's cabinet meeting agendas. They can also become part of regular staff development and mentor program newsletters.

Having a successful project is the second key to generating support. In the words of one project manager from an urban district:

> We seldom get positive press or get a chance to receive state-wide recognition for anything. We

have gotten so much good feedback from this and so much positive attention from the State that the administration is eager to support us.

Some projects have purposely tried to capitalize on the "bandwagon" effect by marketing the project as a model. Others have taken care to appear successful, preparing polished brochures, newsletters, or videotapes.

Providing a valued service is the third way to generate continuing support for new teacher programs. While the success and retention of new teachers is important to all district administrators, it is crucial to the personnel office and to principals. Both urban and rural districts have difficulty competing with the suburbs for fully credentialed new teachers. All districts must compete for good teachers in certain specialty areas. In these instances, providing support to new teachers can be crucial in attracting good applicants. For some districts, it may be the only real marketing advantage they have.

The support of the principal is critical for certain elements of the new teacher project to be successful. The principal is the key to selecting partner teachers, releasing new teachers for observations, and encouraging new teachers to participate in project activities. The traditional scourges of new teachers — multiple preparations, lack of books and materials, problem students, inadequate classrooms, and heavy extracurricular assignments — are often under the principal's control. For all of these reasons, securing the active involvement and support of principals is essential to the success of the program. Similarly, at the secondary level, the backing of department chairs is also important. The Modesto New Teacher Program in particular has found this approach successful.

Avenues to generating support from principals are straightforward. In the words of one program manager, "Principals are eager for our help — it makes their job much easier." In particular, principals welcome orientation assistance during the hectic opening of school. Knowing that someone outside their office can provide individualized support to new faculty is reassuring. They also appreciate having year-round resources to call on when teachers are experiencing particular difficulty. Early involvement of a strong, respected principal in the planning or implementation phase of a new teacher program can also help legitimize the program to other principals.

One note of caution: Some problems can arise from principals, personnel offices, or teachers' associations because of territoriality. While each of these groups are potential allies enthusiastically seeking project assistance, program leaders must be careful to present the project so it is not perceived as infringing on their legitimate functions.

A Final Thought on Collaboration

A successful new teacher support project must have leaders who are adept at crossing organizational boundaries both inside and outside the district. Collaboration is difficult; the greater the numbers of players, the harder it is to maintain communication or simply schedule meetings. Because the individuals involved in the effort are generally open to collaboration and experimentation, they are often overcommitted and have serious time constraints. In addition, tensions between collaborating groups due to collective bargaining, resource allocation, or other issues could harm a new teacher project.

Some steps can be taken to facilitate collaboration and overcome some of these difficulties. The first step entails involving all parties in planning. Hopefully there is enough lead time before program implementation or grant submission for input by all concerned. The second important facilitative step is to make sure all roles are clearly defined in writing to avoid any potential misunderstandings. In the process of role definition, it is important to keep in mind the different strengths and constraints of the organizational partners. These differences can be turned to programmatic advantages by recognizing and building on them. Regular communication and adequate support personnel can keep minor problems from growing and help prevent burn-out. Finally, a good relationship between key project personnel can provide the critical difference between a smooth project and a problematic one. Despite all efforts to facilitate collaboration, problems will arise. When that happens, outside funding or recognition helps keep people going "for the good of the project."

The challenges of education in general, and new teacher preparation and support in particular, defy simplistic approaches. However, the process of collaboration and the creativity that can result from multiple perspectives and resources have the potential to generate the solutions that will be needed to meet the complex challenge within education.

CHAPTER 7

Models of New Teacher Induction Programs

T HIS chapter presents seven models of new teacher induction. The first two programs, *The San Diego State University/San Diego City Unified School District New Teacher Retention Project and the Oakland Unified School District/California State University, Hayward Project New Teacher Support Project* were initiated in 1986. Sponsored by the California State University Chancellor's Office and the State Department of Education, these two programs address the needs of new teachers assigned to inner-city schools through the collaborative efforts of districts and universities.

The remaining five projects are part of the original fifteen programs in the California New Teacher Project which were implemented in 1988. Initiated by the Commission on Teacher Credentialing and the State Department of Education, The California New Teacher Project was designed to establish alternative models of new teacher support and assessment. *Project TAP* (Teacher Assistance Program) represents a university/district collaborative program. *The Santa Cruz Consortium* involves a university, county office of education, and seven school districts. *The Chico Induction for Beginning Teachers Program* is a consortium of a university, several county offices, and school districts in rural northern California. *The Santa Clara Project* is a single-district model for new teacher support. *The Poway Project* is an induction and evaluation model that was initiated by the Poway Federation of Teachers and supported by the local school district.

The models of new teacher support programs that have been presented in this chapter represent only a few of the specific ways in which educational organizations are identifying and addressing the concerns of the beginning teacher in California. The diversity of organization and programming suggest the limitless potential for professional response to the induction needs of new teachers.

SAN DIEGO STATE UNIVERSITY
SAN DIEGO UNIFIED SCHOOL DISTRICT
INNER CITY NEW TEACHER RETENTION PROJECT

The Inner City New Teacher Retention Project is a collaborative program between San Diego State University and the San Diego City Schools. In 1988 the American Association of State Colleges and Universities awarded the project the Christa McAuliffe Showcase for Excellence Award for being an excellent model of large urban school district and university collaboration. The 1989-90 school year marks the fourth year of service provided by the Project to new teachers who teach in multicultural schools in the San Diego Unified School District. To date about 95 percent of the new teachers assisted by the project are still teaching in San Diego schools. Jointly funded by the Chancellor's Office of the California State University system and the Superintendent's Office of the California State Department of Education, the project currently serves 100 beginning teachers a year.

The New Teacher Retention Project represents a developmental and collaborative approach to providing professional growth opportunities as well as an effective support system to new teachers. The project is designed to build on the new teachers' preservice credential preparation, not to supplant it. Project components are designed to acculturate the new teachers as thoughtful practitioners, oriented toward informed decision-making and distinctly capable of translating research and theory into sound professional practice. Project efforts also assist the new teachers in becoming acclimated to their schools and the school district — the context of their professional practice.

Within this conceptual framework, the primary goals of the San Diego Inner City New Teacher Retention Project are:

- to develop an induction year model based on a reflective and analytic conception of teaching;

- to strengthen the instructional effectiveness of new teachers working with students from culturally diverse backgrounds by building on the new teachers' preservice preparation;

- to increase the retention of effective teachers in such settings;

- to provide a formal support network for teachers during the critical transition period of their first year of professional practice; and

- to establish sustained collaboration between San Diego State University and the San Diego Unified School District.

The New Teachers and Their Schools

For the purpose of the program a "new teacher" is defined as a leave replacement or first-year probationary teacher who has had less than six months of teaching experience in any district. For all of these teachers this is their first contract teaching experience. The elementary schools to which these teachers are assigned are in the process of being converted from a traditional school year schedule (September-June) to a year-round schedule composed of four distinct "tracks," wherein classes are staggered in a nine-week-on/three-week-off schedule throughout the calendar year.

For the most part, classes are self-contained and the teachers are responsible for instruction in all subjects of the curriculum. The cultural diversity of the new teachers' classes matches or exceeds overall district patterns of ethnic representation. Among the cultural/ethnic groups represented in the new teachers' classrooms are African-American, Cambodian, Filipino, Hispanic, Indochinese, and Vietnamese.

Program Description

All aspects of the project are jointly planned, reviewed, implemented, and evaluated with leadership provided by co-directors from the university and the school district. Weekly seminars and five release day workshops are presented by individuals from both institutions. Classroom observations and consultations are provided by district mentors, university faculty, and other resource personnel, combining assets from both institutions.

Developing the "Thoughtful Practitioner"

The Retention Project reflects a number of beliefs, shared by the project developers, about both teaching and the types of assistance new teachers need. First, we conceptualize teaching to be a highly complex integration of knowledge and understanding, strategic and technical skills, attitudes and dispositions, analytic and synthesizing capabilities. Second, we believe that the judgments teachers make in practice are pivotal influences on student learning, and that the soundness of these judgments is a function of the depth and richness of these domains. Sound judgment can only be developed within the context of actual practice, but not without shared reflection, assistance, and collegial support. The environment of practice, therefore, must both encourage and value that development. This conception of teaching differs significantly from the narrowly technical and implicitly condescending "teacher-proof" notions embedded in the generic teaching effectiveness prescriptions that have been so pervasive in recent years.

Three key implications for structuring systematic assistance to new teachers follow from this conception. First, recognizing that the new teacher's first teaching assignment constitutes a period of transition, any assistance must address both continued acculturation to the profession (i.e., development of sound judgment, thoughtful informed practice, and a professional self-image defined in terms of these qualities) and acclimatization to the school and school district. Second, the assistance must be structured in such a way that it simultaneously draws out the knowledge and skills the new teacher brings to the enterprise and helps the new teachers contextualize the application and adaptation of that knowledge and those skills to their actual situation. Third, the assistance must encourage the new teachers' confidence in their ability to work through problem situations and to engage with colleagues in shared problem-solving.

In addition to responding to these implications, we have structured the components of the Retention Project to minimize communicating a "survival" mentality to the new teachers, which too often translates to quick fixes for controlling and manipulating students. This concern takes on added poignancy when new teachers are working with culturally diverse populations. Finally, we have been cautious about structuring the content of the project on the basis of the new teachers' perceptions of what they need. We have found their inexperience may lead them to confuse symptoms with problems, and to develop the unrealistic expectation that pre-packaged, universally applicable answers exist. When we do respond to perceived needs, we avoid "doing for" or "doing to" teachers without actively involving their judgment or intellectual engagement.

Program Components

The new teachers are clustered into groups of six to eight persons on the basis of school location and schedule and by grade level if possible (primary, intermediate, middle school). A faculty member from the College of Education serves as the cluster leader and meets with the cluster weekly. Cluster leaders are selected on the basis of their expressed interest in working with new teachers and school district personnel as well as their subject matter and pedagogical expertise. This expertise allows us to build a strong interdisciplinary team.

This organizational structure provides a primary peer support group along with expert assistance. The clusters reduce isolation of new teachers by enriching communication, providing continuity among project participants, and allowing the new teachers to establish important connections with their peers. The cluster leaders work with the new teachers to develop and implement an individualized professional development plan. In addition to planning project activities with other university and school district personnel, the cluster leaders make classroom visits, observations, and demonstrations to new teachers in their clusters and document practices and activities which reflect dimensions or strands of the project.

All the new teachers participate in a year-long series of seminars and workshops that are jointly planned and delivered by university faculty and district personnel. Five thematic strands shape these activities in order to promote the new teachers' professional growth as thoughtful practitioners. These strands include: 1) understanding learners, their individual as well as culturally significant similarities and distinctions; 2) recognizing the importance of such understanding in developing and implementing both instruction and management effectively; 3) continuing to expand and deepen subject matter understanding as a strategy for increasing the likelihood that curriculum is accurately and meaningfully addressed; 4) expanding the new teachers' repertoire of instructional approaches as well as enriching their capability for adapting and adjusting approaches given variability in learnings and learners; 5) developing the complex cognitive capabilities, particularly analytical and synthesizing skills, which underlie informed professional practice. Within the context of these strands, presentations are made in such topics as classroom management, professional growth planning, stress management, cultural diversity, cooperative education, reciprocal teaching, writing as a process, the preparation of case reports, and instructional strategies in the content areas of language arts, math, science, social studies, and fine arts.

Following the whole group seminar presentation and a question-and-answer period, the new teachers meet in their clusters and write for ten minutes about any significant incident that happened during the week. This strategy affords the new teachers an opportunity to reflect on what they and their students are doing, why events are happening as they are, what pleases them and what they want to sustain as well as change in the classroom. The critical incidents are not necessarily just a reporting of problems or negative events, because new teachers also write

about progress they are having in an area of concern, events that have boosted their self-confidence, or flashes of insight that writing helps them preserve. The new teachers are not required to share what they have written with their peers in the seminar. They do, however, turn them in to their cluster leader for written response or comments. This routine provides a systematic means of confidential communication and permits regular opportunities for contact between cluster leaders and the new teachers. The cluster leaders report that a review of the weekly critical incidents alerts them to the need for individual assistance with the new teachers and to instances of new teachers who confuse symptoms with problems.

The discussion portion of the seminar becomes an extension of the critical writing incident and can take a number of directions depending on the needs and interests of the group. Sharing experiences, commiserating, problem sharing and solving take up much of the time in these sessions. The discussions provide collaborative opportunities for the new teachers to reflect on their practice and work through problems together. The cluster leaders facilitate these discussions and encourage new teachers to think broadly about alternative solutions to identified problems.

Critical incident writing promotes reflection about teaching and provides the new teachers an opportunity to be thoughtful about their practice while dealing with the practical real life world of their classrooms. From these critical incidents the new teachers are required to write two case reports, one each semester, on incidents they feel are particularly influential in their thinking and development as a professional.

The new teachers submit an initial draft of their case report which is read by the cluster leaders and returned with comments, suggestions, and questions intended to prompt greater elaboration or depth of consideration. At this point, the case report becomes the basis for professional dialogue between the "reader" (in this case, the cluster leader) and the new teacher about the new teacher's thinking and her/his representation of it. The new teachers are encouraged to refine their dialogue through successive drafts, as time, energy, and interest permit. Final drafts are turned in following this process. The procedure is repeated during the writing of the second case report, with the addition of commentaries solicited from colleagues or site administrators. These commentaries help give the new teachers another interpretation of the incidents from which they are drawn.

Through the new teachers' accounts of their experience, we can see that they do not enter the profession as "blank slates." The critical incidents and case reports reveal the thoughts of people who are trying to sustain their beliefs and synthesize their knowledge about teaching and learning within the context of complex teaching situations. Included in the critical incidents and case reports are burgeoning philosophical statements reflecting the application of theory and beliefs which emanate from their knowledge of psychology, sociology, content material, and their knowledge of the world of "school."

The release day workshops (five throughout the year) usually focus on a topic fairly new to the teachers and therefore require a longer concentration of time. Familiarizing the new teachers with the school district curriculum, related materials and resources, for example, was one release day topic, as was cooperative learning strategies. The release days afford the teachers the opportunity to try some things out in the safe and helpful company of colleagues. Mentor teachers often participate in the release days with the new teachers, frequently as presenters or demonstrators.

Through the California Mentor Teacher Program, each new teacher is matched with a mentor teacher from the school district. These matches are made on the basis of similarity in grade, curriculum and student assignments. The mentor teachers provide classroom visitation and consultation assistance to the new teachers. They also serve as presenters in the seminars and workshops.

Through meetings with project administrators, the mentors come to understand and contribute to the conception of teaching underpinning the project. To the new teachers, the mentors personify credibility. They represent successful practice, ability, even virtuosity in what the new teacher is about to try. They possess the knowledge of the district as a distinct culture; they know how it works. They demonstrate the seasoned and balanced perspective which encourages risk-taking and engenders stability.

The new teachers are also provided a network of resource personnel from both the university and school district. In addition to serving as seminar presenters,

these individuals provide classroom consultations to individual new teachers and assist them in becoming acclimated to the school district, its resources, policies, and operating procedures. Coordination of this support network is provided by the school district's Office of Staff Development and Training. In particular, the office assigns one of its resource teachers half-time to the Retention Project. This person serves as a critical liaison between the new teachers and the various administrative and resource departments of the school district. He also fills a key planning and logistics role in the development of all facets of the project.

The project provides the new teachers with scholarships for six units of graduate credit at the San Diego State University. These units are earned through participation in the seminars and release days, and through successful completion of course requirements. The units are applicable for salary advancement and can be counted toward the state's requirement of 150 hours of continuing education every five years. An instructional materials stipend of between $200 and $300 is available to each new teacher as well. The project also provides for five release days throughout the school year for the new teachers and the school district provides five release days for their mentor teachers.

Project Administration

The dean of the San Diego State University College of Education serves as Principal Investigator and provides overall policy and programmatic direction to the project. The project has two co-directors: the Director of San Diego Unified School District's Office of Staff Development and Training, and a faculty member from the San Diego State University School of Teacher Education. A half-time resource teacher, a full-time secretary, and a student assistant also provide vital support to the Retention Project. These individuals meet regularly to discuss and evaluate the project. In addition, the San Diego State University co-director meets weekly with the cluster leaders.

Project Changes, Observations, and Concluding Thoughts

The New Teacher Retention Project represents a true collaboration between the San Diego Unified School District and San Diego State University. While the collaboration takes a considerable amount of time and personal energy, it provides opportunities for shared ownership, access to broader professional resources, and substantial impact on the professional development of new teachers that no other arrangements would afford. The collaborative element is considered essential to the project's success in bringing theory and application together.

In the four years since the New Teacher Retention Project was implemented, three significant modifications have been incorporated into the program design: 1) adopting the cluster structure instead of a large group approach to interacting with new teachers; 2) incorporating critical incidents and case reports as strategies for promoting thoughtful practice and evaluating new teacher professional growth; and 3) broadening the involvement of university faculty in the program. Rationale for the first two modifications has been presented earlier; however, the purpose for broadening the involvement of university faculty warrants further discussion.

In the first year of the project, university participation was limited to the project director who participated in the weekly seminars, and several content area consultants who visited new teachers' classrooms upon request. This year, eight university faculty members serve as cluster leaders. Their participation in the project has had a significant socializing effect on both the new teachers and the university educators. The weekly dialogue that occurs in the cluster groups provides faculty with the opportunity to add cognitive and experiential breadth and depth to the collaborative analysis of the teaching experience. The critical incident/case report approach promotes new teacher participation in what might be considered "an apprenticeship in analysis." Concurrently, faculty members gain increased insights into the often stark realities of teaching in the inner-city schools as new teachers share their stories. This knowledge has an impact on the preservice programs.

After several years of working in this collaborative effort, it is abundantly clear that the project is very important to new teachers. The provision of the support network and activities, coupled with thoughtful reflection on their own experiences, promotes attending to the immediate and practical needs of classroom teaching while simultaneously developing habits of mind and practice that will sustain these teachers well beyond the first year. This continuity of

reflection, the notion of the "thoughtful practitioner," will support professional teachers as they enter their second year and throughout their career.

— Prepared by Ann I. Morey and Diane S. Murphy

San Diego State University/ San Diego City Schools New Teacher Retention Project Staff

Project Director University Co-Director (1989 —)	Ann I. Morey Diane S. Murphy
Past University Co-Director (1987-1989)	Mary Gendernalik Cooper
District Co-Director	Mary Hopper
Resource Teacher	Rich Biffle
Project Secretary	Susie Kidder

Contact Person:
Dr. Diane S. Murphy
New Teacher Retention Project
San Diego State University
San Diego, California 92182
(619) 594-2890

THE OAKLAND-CALIFORNIA STATE UNIVERSITY, HAYWARD NEW TEACHER SUPPORT PROJECT

This project began in 1986-87 as a pilot to increase the retention and effectiveness of beginning teachers in inner-city Oakland. Jointly funded by the Chancellor's Office of the California State University and the California State Department of Education, it initially served 25 teachers. Now in its fourth year, the project provides varying levels of support to all non-tenured teachers in Oakland.

Over the four years the elements of new teacher support have remained the same: *release time* to observe other teachers or visit resource centers; a *teacher consultant* on site to provide psychological support, instructional guidance, and orientation; a *university consultant* from the Hayward Department of Teacher Education offering clinical supervision and a link to professional practices beyond the District; *wider university support from other disciplines* as the need arises; *workshops* where teachers can form a support group and receive helpful classroom materials and ideas; and *stipends* for the purchase of instructional materials. However, as the project has matured, the content and delivery of this support has changed; so too has the management structure of the project and the district-university relationship.

Evolution of Project Elements

Release Time. Under the original pilot design, teachers were released one day a week for observation, seminars, planning, and visitations. This weekly absence from their classrooms proved too frequent, causing classroom management problems as well as difficulties in providing substitutes. In the second year teachers were only released every other week; still, the problems arose. Nonetheless, release time was the most highly rated project element both years. In the third and fourth years of the New Teacher Support Project participants were granted substitutes for six days, which has proven to be a more appropriate number, given the lack of reliable, quality substitutes.

Teacher Consultants. All participating teachers were paired with experienced teachers at their school sites. These experienced teachers provided crisis support, practical and political advice, and curricular guidance. In the third and fourth years they received coaching training and three release days to work with the new teachers. They were also allocated a stipend.

In 1986-87 principals selected the teacher consultants with mixed success. Some did not know the new teachers well enough to make good matches; others selected consultants on a political basis. In 1987-88 the new teachers chose their own consultants, again with mixed results. Many were too new to teaching or to their faculty to make appropriate choices. In the last two years, participants have nominated one or two consultants, with final selection being made by the principal. This new selection procedure, coupled with training and release time, has generally increased the efficacy of the teacher consultants.

A second change related to teacher consultants occurred in year three, when the project went district-wide. During the first two years it proved impossible to select teacher consultants before mid-October. At the same time, program evaluation targeted September as the time when new teachers most needed assistance. To address this disparity, in years three and four the Mentor Bridge was instituted. At hire, the Bridge paired district mentors with new teachers to offer general support until the more carefully matched teacher consultants could be put in place. Later these mentors were on call for any non-tenured teacher needing special assistance.

University Consultants. The university consultant has been the primary project resource providing in-class observation and clinical supervision to new teachers. Hayward Teacher Education faculty observe participants biweekly on a regular university supervision formula. Great care has been taken to establish a consultative, teacher-directed relationship rather than a supervisorial or evaluative one. Over the past four years the only change in this aspect of the program has been an increase in the ratio of new teachers to university consultants, from 15:1 to 25:1. Made for financial reasons, this change did affect the quality of consultation. Even so, the evaluation of university consultants remained high.

Wider University Consultation. In its original conception, the New Teacher Support Project was to draw upon the expertise of the wider university faculty for curricular assistance. This goal has been very successfully met on the secondary level, especially in the sciences. It has proven elusive at the elementary level, however. University professors from outside the School of Education have generally had difficulties translating their content in ways that would be directly applicable to an elementary classroom.

Workshops. In its first two years the project held formal biweekly seminars for university credit. These offered a combination of theoretical and hands-on presentations. While participants appreciated the interaction with each other and with seminar leaders, they found the formal nature of the course, and its frequency, too demanding. Therefore, in years three and four the seminars became the less formal Elementary and Secondary New Teacher Networks. These monthly meetings featured mentor-led workshops on specific, pragmatic instructional strategies and materials. Response to the change has been positive.

Stipends. Early in the project it was found that new teachers were significantly constrained by their lack of classroom materials, particularly since they were teaching at severely underfunded inner-city schools. To address this need, $200 was allocated to each participant ($150 in year four). In general the monies were well spent and strongly boosted morale.

University Involvement

The original impetus and primary first-year leadership for the New Teacher Support Project came from the California State University, Hayward. The university's strong role evolved primarily because its politics and structures differed from those of the district. Basically, it was easier to buy university faculty time than the time of a district administrator. The ability to devote time exclusively to the project was critical during the start-up phase – not just to get the project going, but also to produce the kind of success and visibility necessary to insure district support and commitment. In year two NTSP leadership became more shared, and in year three – when the project expanded to serve more than 200 teachers – day-to-day management transferred to the district. At this point, a mentor teacher on leave was hired as the full-time manager. Finally, in year four, financial efficiency prompted the dividing of project management among four mentor teachers who did not receive release time. They formed a leadership team with the district and university directors. By year four, the university director was involved primarily in the development of project spin-offs rather than management of the on-going program.

New Directions

Over the first three years of the project it became increasingly apparent that new inner-city teachers needed intense site-level support. In particular, they needed to begin their careers in a highly professional environment where their colleagues were committed to on-going professional growth. Unfortunately, such assignments for new teachers are rare. Therefore, in year three the NTSP began working with two elementary schools, one predominantly black and the other black and Hispanic, to design professional development schools. Faculty from each site spent nearly a year visiting other schools, reading research, and planning their programs. Each redesigned its organizational structure, dividing into cooperating grade-level teams. In addition, each school developed a specific curricular focus, a comprehensive schedule of staff development, and a commitment to peer coaching. This fall (1989-90), three-quarter time interns were assigned to work with each teacher as part of an urban/minority teacher recruitment program.

Next year positions will be set aside at each school for two-year residency contracts for fully credentialed beginning teachers. In addition, minority instructional aides with an interest in pursuing full teaching credentials will be given preference for instructional aide positions at each school.

Summary

The Oakland-CSU Hayward New Teacher Support Project has evolved from a university-centered project serving 25 new teachers at approximately $8,000 each to a dual-focus effort involving two different types of district-university partnerships. The first, the continuing district-wide New Teacher Support Project, is now district-run and serving up to 150 new teachers at $1,200 to $1,900 each. The university plays a supportive role in this process. The second focus, the development of two induction/professional development schools, has a heavy initial university involvement in partnership with site-level teachers and administrators. Both aspects of the project demonstrate the fluid, dynamic nature of successful district-university collaboration. Each partner has a different role to play, depending upon the nature of the task and the developmental phase of the program.

— prepared by Louise Bay Waters, Project Director

The Oakland-California State University, Hayward New Teacher Support Project

District Project Director   Cynthia Harris
University Project Director   Louise Bay Waters
Management Team   Dolores Godbold
                         Maria Watson
                         Ernie Miller
                         Evelyn Ely

Contact Person:
Louise Bay Waters
Project Director
New Teacher Support Project
California State University, Hayward
Hayward, California 94542
(415) 881-3009

Poway Professional Assistance Program

Program Overview

There is little disagreement within our educational community that beginning teachers must make a difficult adjustment as they move from the academic world to the real world of the classroom. The quality of the teacher work force is influenced not only by who enters teaching, but by who stays in teaching. By the beginning of the next century we will have to replace half of our nation's 2.2 million teachers due to retirement (the average age of teachers is 47) and attrition (50 percent of teachers leave after only five years in the profession, 80 percent are gone after ten years). Just as alarming are the figures relating to able college students choosing teaching as a profession. In 1973 almost 20 percent of college graduates considered teaching as a career; today that figure has plummeted to 7 percent. The resulting shortage of new, promising teachers is not just a problem particular to personnel directors. It is of significance to everyone concerned with effective schools.

Fully responsible for instruction of his/her students from the first working day, the beginning teacher performs the same tasks as a 20-year veteran. We in the profession often short-change our "rookies." Tasks are not added sequentially to allow for gradual increase in skill and knowledge; the beginner learns while performing the full complement of teaching duties. Since teaching style is most often developed early in a teacher's career, it is particularly important to monitor teachers' early work in the classroom. In most schools, supervision of the new teacher is rare, limited to infrequent and brief observations of classroom performance. The Poway Unified School District and the Poway Federation of Teachers, the local teachers' union, agreed that intensive supervision, training and support for new teachers was imperative and mutually beneficial to both organizations.

The Poway Professional Assistance Program (PPAP) was based on this mutual recognition of needs and the premise that experienced teachers have a legitimate role in the screening and training of new entrants into the profession. This teacher induction and assessment system provides teachers new to Poway with the services of an experienced classroom teacher to help them ease into their new professional roles. The experienced teacher, called a teacher consultant, has a workload of 12 to 15 teachers and assumes the responsibility for the first-year evaluation of each of those teachers. The teacher consultant provides each new teacher with thorough and frequent classroom observations, assistance, objective criticism, coaching and supervision from a recognized expert teacher.

The teacher consultant periodically reports the progress of the new teachers to the Peer Review Board. This board, composed of union and administrative representatives, monitors the work of the consultants and governs the program under the umbrella of a trust agreement. It is this board that accepts or rejects the final evaluative findings of the consultants and forwards its recommendation to the superintendent of schools and ultimately to the school board of trustees. This unique collaborative effort between the union and the district has been a fundamental departure from past relationships and has set a cornerstone for further local reform.

The evaluation aspect is unique, but the program is more than peer review. The consultants' work with the new teachers begins with the planning and presentations of New Teacher Day and continues throughout the year. The consultants view their role as one of support and assistance for the new teacher rather than one of evaluation. From explaining the spelling program, modeling a classroom management strategy, providing a sympathetic ear, and explaining the social and political expectations of the staff room, to administering a strong dose of reality, the teacher consultant provides a resource heretofore unavailable to teachers new to Poway.

The District

The Poway Unified School District (PUSD) is located in the west central portion of San Diego County approximately 25 miles north of San Diego and 10 miles from the Pacific Ocean. The district's boundaries encompass 103 square miles and include the city of Poway and the city of San Diego, plus a small portion of unincorporated territory in the county of San Diego.

Three major communities are located in the PUSD. The Poway community is largely residential in character with a moderately expanding commercial segment. Rancho Bernardo, a planned community, includes a 635-acre industrial park which contains some of the nation's largest firms. Rancho Peñasquitos is also a planned community which is almost exclusively residential in character with limited commercial development.

The overall community is predominantly a white, middle class community with 72 percent of the families classified as professional or semi-professional, as contrasted with 33 percent in these classifications statewide. The racial/ethnic composition of district students is 83.8 percent white and a 16.2 percent minority mix of Asian/Pacific Islander, Filipino, black and Hispanic.

The Poway Federation of Teachers has been the local bargaining agent for the teachers since 1976. Contract negotiations have been stormy at best and the relationship between the union and district has fluctuated from distant and strained to cool and professional. Because of the success at jointly managing the PPAP, both parties agreed in 1988 to attempt contract negotiations using a non-adversarial model. They were successful in negotiating a two-year contract ready for ratification upon the teachers' return in September, an event that has only happened once in the previous 18 years.

The Teacher Consultant

Early in the planning stages of the program, both the union and the administration agreed on some guidelines for developing the new position of teacher consultant. Although the consultant is in some ways similar to a mentor teacher, it was recognized that the consultant's responsibilities would far exceed those of a mentor. It was decided that the position should be full time, so that each of the consultants would be released from classroom duties to work exclusively with the new teachers. However, it was also recognized that the consultant's role needed to be viewed by all staff as that of "expert teacher" rather than as one experienced staff member put it, "a training ground for junior administrators." It was thus decided to limit the term for each individual consultant to three consecutive years, after which the consultant returns to the classroom for a period of at least one year. The consultant would remain in the teacher bargaining unit and would receive the same monetary stipend and district status as a mentor teacher.

Applicants for the position must have five years of district experience and apply for announced vacancies. The selection is completed by a joint teacher/

administrator panel following a writing sample, interviews, recommendations of teachers and administrators and, if needed, classroom observations. Experience showed that the degree of flexibility for potential assignments by grade level or subject matter was important, so the breadth of previous teaching experience of the applicant proved to be significant. Personal skills, such as the ability to communicate and to be sympathetic are critical attributes.

The teacher consultant position has been evolving over the past two years.

Experience during the past two years has enabled the teacher consultant to anticipate and help the new teacher avoid beginning-of-school problems such as difficulty adjusting to late assignment changes, feelings of isolation at the site, and trouble accessing furniture and supplies. The consultants share a program goal of being in each of their new teachers' classrooms a minimum of once a week. They must complete at least 20 hours of contact time for each of two evaluation periods. This is 20 times the contractual requirement used prior to the program, although the evaluation process is not emphasized during the month of September. Time in the classroom and time conferencing is critical to the success of the consultant.

The consultant, working with the site administrator and under the supervision of the Peer Review Board, assists each new teacher on an individual basis. By placing the consultant in the novice's classroom on a frequent basis, the program is able to provide the new teacher with staff development at an appropriate time in the learning cycle. If the new teacher is ready to focus on curriculum concerns, it makes little sense for all new teachers to attend mandated inservices on cooperative learning. Conversely, the consultant may elect to attend an inservice in CAP writing with a new high school English teacher and work with that teacher to implement CAP strategies in the classroom. The consultant frequently models instructional strategies in the new teacher's classroom or releases the new teacher to visit the classrooms of other skilled professionals.

Each consultant receives the usual training in the technical skills used in the evaluation of teachers. Additionally, each consultant has $500 available for his own professional development. The team of consultants meets formally once a week to share ideas, receive advice on a teacher facing some difficulty, arrange calendars and "recharge batteries." Isolation, loss of the love and contact with their own classrooms and a difficult assignment may be drawbacks to the consultant assignment. Informal meetings and networking by telephone have proven to be invaluable resources.

Formative and summative evaluations on each consultant are completed by one union and one administrative representative of the Peer Board of Review. Each new teacher and each principal is surveyed. Interviews also provide data for the evaluation.

Program costs are the salary of the consultant's classroom replacement, the consultant stipend, and miscellaneous minor support costs. In Poway, the 1989-90 cost is about $34,000 per consultant position (taking into account all monies spent).

Peer Evaluation

The PPAP based its program on the research work of Arthur Wise, Linda Darling-Hammond, Milbrey McLaughlin, and Harriet Bernstein in the 1984 Rand Corporation study on teacher evaluation and the work started in Toledo, Ohio. These authors surveyed evaluation practices in a number of districts and offered several observations that were incorporated into the PPAP. We believe that teacher involvement and responsibility improve the quality of teacher evaluation. Our program recognized that the responsibilities of the site principal require that she try to be all things to all teachers. But the teacher consultant role is focused only on the new teacher. The increased time and the narrowing focus greatly strengthens the district's capacity to effectively supervise new teachers. Because the consultants are practitioners of what they preach, they have great credibility with their teachers.

Involving the teacher's union in the design and oversight of new teacher evaluation helped ensure legitimacy, fairness and effectiveness. The minimum of 20 hours of assistance and assessment per evaluation period is far exceeded with teachers facing some difficulty, and in one case, involved over 100 hours of contact time by more than one consultant. The Peer Review Board accepted the recommendation of the consultant not to renew the contract of the new teacher, and the union was part of that process. The best way for a union to ensure that new teachers

receive due process and all the assistance possible is to jointly govern and monitor a program that provides that service. Only six of the 110 teachers participating in the program over the last two years have not been rehired for their second probationary year.

The Review Board also recognized that role conflict between administrators and teachers would be inevitable, but by being sensitive to specific concerns the impact of those conflicts could be minimized. The program was made optional for each site principal. The expectation was that some administrators would be reluctant to give up the evaluation process at first, but would be convinced as the program matured. This expectation was met. During the first year about 60 percent of the schools participated in the program using peer review, the second year included almost all the schools, and the third year all schools with new teachers are participating in the program. By constantly communicating with the site principal and encouraging that person to make frequent, informal "drop-in" visits to the new teacher's classroom, the consultant ensures that the needs of the site administration are met.

The Peer Review Board and Trust Agreement

The program is governed by the Peer Review Board composed of the Federation president and two other union representatives plus the Assistant Superintendent in personnel and an additional administrative representative. This board meets about every six to eight weeks, or as specifically needed. A majority vote is deemed to be four votes. Consultants report the progress of each of their new teachers and the Board may recommend several alternative strategies or plans to improve the performance of the new teacher. Budgeting decisions, personnel choices, evaluation and the assignments of the consultants are all functions of the Peer Review Board.

The Federation of Teachers and the district operate the project under the umbrella of a trust agreement that both parties renew annually. A trust agreement is a negotiated compact between a district and a union. Trust agreements are intended to specify educational problems of joint concern and establish mechanisms for working on them. They set aside money, time and authority and they create structures that allow union and management to resolve disputes as they work toward joint goals. Trust agreements anticipate joint action on problems such as curriculum reform, student achievement, teaching careers, school restructuring, and teacher evaluation. Technically, they are frequently beyond the scope of bargaining for labor contracts. The Poway trust agreement is only one of six such agreements operating in California.

The trust agreement enabled the working relationship of the Review Board to set a new benchmark for labor relations in Poway. The cooperation and mutual respect necessary for the success of the program are beginning to be seen in other programs throughout the district. This is a pleasant but not unexpected byproduct of the process.

Program Review

The PPAP has contracted for an independent review/evaluation from San Diego State University, and copies of the reports from 1987-88 and 1988-89 are available. The program has evolved using recommendations from the previous years. Many of these recommendations were procedural rather than conceptual but the most significant of these dealt with peer evaluation.

During the initial pilot year (1987-88) the consultants were working with new teachers at some schools where the principal wanted the consultant to assist but not evaluate the new teacher. The evaluator found that the consultants were less effective with teachers at those sites than with teachers at sites where the consultants were evaluators. This was especially true with new teachers who were struggling in the classroom. For future years the Review Board chose to continue to make the program optional for principals but ensured that the consultants were the sole evaluators. All but two principals opted for the program the second year, and in the third year all schools are participating.

The program applied for and received inclusion in the California New Teacher Project beginning in the 1988-89 school year. An additional consultant was hired (bringing the total to four), but timing forced this new person to be hired after the start of school. This proved to be a great disruption for students, new teachers and especially the new consultant. Anticipating a similar problem, the Review Board formed a "pool" of five possible consultants in June of 1989 that would be immediately available to start in September of the new school year.

The consultants' view of the operation of the district is somewhat global, since they work in classrooms at every school. It appears that this is a unique experience among all district staff. There seems to be some diversity between schools, and some of these differences significantly affected the new teachers. For example, during the first year only ten percent of the new teachers were satisfied with the equipment in their classrooms and the instructional supplies available. But then the consultants began reporting to the Review Board and quietly working with principals; the level of teacher satisfaction in the second year rose to 57 percent. The consultants also convinced the staff development director to change the format used for "New Teacher Day," which traditionally was a morning devoted to greetings by administrators and a guest speaker. In the past two years the time allocated to administrators decreased and no guest lecturers were invited to speak. Instead the new teachers are broken up into grade level groups led by experienced teacher experts that help introduce the curriculum – "the way we do things here in Poway" – and who help locate resources. Although allowing time for teachers to speak together may seem simplistic, it was a novel recommendation that has proven to be a great success.

Finally, the issue of which new teachers may participate in the program is still a concern that needs to be addressed. Poway has more teachers new to the district than the program's resources can accommodate. Currently, the program is serving all new teachers who have less than two years' experience in the field of education. However, a district study has revealed that new hires who have had experience in other districts may still need to be served by this program. In fact, 50 percent of the teachers dropped from the program came to Poway with several years of experience. The principals and consultants have had some difficulty deciding on which "experienced" new teachers should be recommended to the Review Board for inclusion in the program.

Plans for Expansion

Plans for expansion of the Poway Professional Assistance Program fall into three areas. The union would very much like all teachers new to the district, regardless of experience or assignment, to be included in the program. For this year that would mean the addition of three full-time consultants. Not a trivial cost! The program is also planning some type of activity for second year teachers. PPAP provides a great deal of close supervision during the first probationary year and believes some type of "bridging" program is needed for the second year. Finally, it seems desirable to use the services of the recognized teaching expert, the consultant, in a non-evaluative manner to assist a permanent employee facing serious professional jeopardy. The 1989-90 school year will be used to plan these activities.

The benefits of the Poway Professional Assistance Program for the new teacher, the district, and the profession are many, but it is the students of Poway who will reap the ultimate rewards.

— Prepared by Donald Raczka

Poway Professional Assistance Program Staff

Project Coordinator/	
Teacher Consultant	Donald Raczka
Teacher Consultant	Christine Evans
Teacher Consultant	Charlotte Kutzner
Teacher Consultant	Veleta Rollins
Teacher Consultant	Janet Malone
Program Evaluator	Barbara Moore

Contact Person:
Donald Raczka
Project Coordinator
Poway Professional Assistance Program
14640 Tierra Bonita Road
Poway, California 92064
(619) 748-0010 ext. 283

CALIFORNIA STATE UNIVERSITY, CHICO INDUCTION FOR THE BEGINNING TEACHER PROGRAM

The Induction for the Beginning Teacher Program is a comprehensive and innovative program of support and skill-building designed to assist beginning teachers in rural Northern California in making the transition from effective students to effective teachers, and ultimately to retain them in the profession. Program participants receive comprehensive instruction in targeted skills through seminars delivered on the California State University, Chico, campus and over instructional television. The program pairs each beginning teacher with a successful, experienced teacher trained in peer coaching and observation techniques. Each pair forms a teaching team that develops action-research plans for implementing

seminar concepts in the beginning teacher's classroom. The experienced teacher-peer coach observes, supports, and provides feedback to his/her beginning teacher on a weekly basis.

The program has been deemed highly successful by its participants and their administrators. This success is due largely to its comprehensive and individualistic structure, and to the fact that the program has been able to meet the needs of teachers in isolated two-teacher schools, as well as the teachers in the "emerging urban" schools of the Chico university's vast 36,000 square mile area (almost the size of the state of Ohio). The conceptual framework and components of the Induction for the Beginning Teacher Program are described below.

Conceptual Framework

Teaching is a complex profession. Yet, traditionally, new teachers are required to perform the same tasks, at the same level of competence, as the seasoned professional. Recent literature and empirical research on beginning teachers indicate that many aspects of teaching cannot be learned or experienced during the university preservice program. Some aspects of teaching *can only be experienced as an individual becomes a new teacher — alone in the classroom.* Consequently, beginning teachers often report:

- Feelings of isolation and insecurity

- Problems with classroom management

- Lack of skills in evaluating students and communicating with parents

- A basic inability to blend into the social structure of the school

Without guidance, support, technical assistance, and supervision, beginning teachers may resort to survival techniques that rely on teaching methods that are likely to prevent their developing into effective teachers. For some, poor performance evaluations lead to job dissatisfaction and early career changes. It is clear that many new teachers leave the profession when their frustrations peak, *resulting in an attrition rate of almost 40 percent of all teachers by their second year* (The Governor's 1991 Report on Education, p. 37). Even more alarming is the evidence that the best teachers may be the first to leave.

Project Development. New teacher retention is a major concern of the rural isolated areas of Northern California. Some counties report that 100 percent of their new teachers who come from outside their geographic areas leave the profession before they have completed two years of teaching.

This fact and many others surfaced during a needs assessment conducted during the 1986-87 academic year by the California State University, Chico's Institute for Advanced Studies in Education. This assessment included interviews with local educators in the 14 rural counties of the university's 36,000 square mile service area as well as a detailed review of the literature and a national interactive teleconference designed to identify issues and solutions related to beginning teachers. Following the evaluation of the data collected, it was determined that there was a need for a program that promoted good teaching, supported new teachers, and encouraged these beginning professionals to remain in the profession.

California State University, Chico faculty member, Dr. Victoria Bernhardt, in collaboration with university faculty members and teachers and administrators from the university's service region developed the *Induction for the Beginning Teacher Program*. The design and content of the program was widely reviewed in open forums by university faculty and county and district educators within the service region.

The program was pre-tested during the 1987-88 academic year. Pleased that the design of the program reflected their input, and confident that it had the potential to meet the needs of their beginning teachers, districts demonstrated their support and commitment by collectively absorbing a portion of the direct "bare-bones" costs of the pilot program. These districts also provided release time for teachers to participate in the program and for teachers and administrators to serve on the Advisory Committee.

During the 1988-89 academic year, the Induction for the Beginning Teacher Program became one of the fifteen projects funded by the California State Department of Education and the Commission on Teacher Credentialing through the California New Teacher Project.

Philosophy and Goals. The underlying philosophy of the program is that beginning teachers already have the basic tools they need for developing into successful, long-term teachers. What they need is a support program which allows them to grow into the profession — a safety net for experimentation, evaluation, and reflection.

The goals of the Induction for the Beginning Teacher Program are to provide a support and information system that will:

- improve instructional abilities,

- promote self-assessment and reflection,

- enhance working conditions and job satisfaction by reducing professional and geographic isolation,

- model professionalism and provide opportunities for professional growth,

- increase teacher retention rates while retaining the best teachers, and

- provide the best educational experience for school age children.

Structures for Implementation

The structure of the Induction for the Beginning Teacher Program has been modified over time to meet the changing needs of the service area. However, the basic structure has remained constant and has been proven to be an effective and appropriate model for the induction of beginning teachers. In essence:

- Each beginning teacher is paired with a successful experienced teacher, preferably from the same grade level, content area, and school. This pair forms a teaching team.

- The experienced teacher is trained by the program in peer coaching and observation techniques.

- The teaching team attends monthly seminars both on-campus and at local *Instructional Television for Students* sites. This is the Chico university's interactive microwave television system that links the campus to the 14 Northern California counties in its service region. It allows participants to view the program from their counties without having to drive up to six hours to attend all sessions on campus.

- Following each monthly seminar, each teaching team develops an action-research plan for implementing the seminar's concepts in the beginning teacher's classroom.

- Peer coaches observe their beginning teachers on a weekly basis, either in person or on videotape, to reinforce the implementation of the action-research plan.

- Following each observation, the beginning teacher and peer coach hold a post-observation conference to review the successful elements of the beginning teacher's performance, and to plan the next logical step.

This structure enables the teaching team to focus on specific skills after each seminar. The teaching team plans together for this learning, and participates as a team in implementing the plan, evaluating the results, and projecting future action. Effort is devoted to identifying successful experiences, allowing the beginning teacher to learn from what he/she is doing right. This structure offers safety to the beginning teachers so that they may experiment and find sound instructional techniques that work for them.

Roles of Experienced Educators

Experienced teachers (peer coaches) are the backbone of the Chico university's induction program. They provide instruction, collegiality, feedback, and support to beginning teachers where they need it — back in their classrooms. The support, insight, and safety provided by experienced teachers are regarded as essential to the learning of beginning teachers. The specific duties of the peer coaches are to:

- attend each seminar with the beginning teachers,

- extend the seminar learning into the classrooms,

- assist beginning teachers in the development of action-research plans,

- oversee implementation of the plans, and

- provide supportive and constructive feedback after each weekly observation.

The peer coach's knowledge of the beginning teacher and the situation in which that teacher is performing enable her/him to offer insight and suggestions that are tailored to immediate individual needs. In this way, seminar concepts can be carried to the "grass-roots" level.

Instructional and administrative staff reinforce the comprehensiveness of the program structure. Staff make site visits to the schools of participating beginning teachers where they observe and conference with the participants and meet with their administrators. Individually tailored instruction and technical assistance to the teaching team are provided. In addition, feedback from program participants is obtained and used to further refine seminar offerings to address the current needs of beginning teachers. Program staff are able to see first-hand the teaching conditions each participant must confront. Thus, they are able to suggest alternative strategies to individual participants that will help mitigate negative conditions and capitalize on positive ones. Seminar offerings are also fine-tuned to reflect this input. In this way, program staff are able to extend personal support and validation to the new teacher as an important and valued member of the profession.

Content Emphasized

Program content emphasizes positive, constructive issues which help beginning teachers sort out the difference between a problem and a condition, and identify how to respond appropriately to each. Content areas are selected based on a synthesis of research and are presented in an activities-oriented approach. Content includes:

Classroom Management: Creating a Positive Classroom Environment
Classroom Management: Developing and Implementing a Discipline Plan
Classroom Management: Understanding Your Power and How to Use It
Time Management: Balancing Personal and Professional Commitments
Implementing Model Curriculum Standards in Your Lessons

Student Evaluation and Motivation
Teaching Students Who are At Risk
Teacher as Instructional Leader
Coaching Teachers to Higher Levels of Effectiveness (for peer coaches)

These topics were chosen on the basis of the needs assessment that was conducted in the design phase of the program and through a survey of the participating first-year teachers. They were the most frequently mentioned in the literature and by professional educators (both experienced educators and new teachers) as areas of difficulty for beginning teachers. Thus, these topics serve as a sound instructional base for the program as well as a viable springboard for the action planning and "learn by doing" support that are integral to the success of the participants.

Program seminars focus on the identification of individual talents and teaching styles and an exploration of how each might be used effectively. In addition, beginning teachers are encouraged to explore different styles as potential adaptations that might be useful in a variety of classroom settings. Emphasis is placed on refining what the beginning teacher does well and introducing variations on these strategies as a way of generating options so that he/she gains confidence and a realistic perspective as well as a set of educationally sound techniques.

Modifications to the Project

Over the past two years of operation, the Induction for the Beginning Teacher Program has been responsive to the reactions and input of program participants and their administrators. Thus, a second year follow-up program has been designed to offer continued growth opportunities for new teachers. This phase of the program deals in depth with identification of individual learning styles and the teaching of students who are at risk. In addition, two administrative workshops are being offered to give administrators a greater understanding of the program and peer coaching. The topics of these workshops will be Coaching Teachers to Higher Levels of Excellence, and Evaluations That Make a Difference.

Two books have been written to augment and document important aspects of the program (see Bernhardt and Triplett, Flaherty and Rebello, in the Resource Section of this document).

Annual program evaluations clearly demonstrate that the Induction for the Beginning Teacher Program strongly influences the early professional development of beginning teachers. Beginning teachers have consistently improved their classroom performances according to the observations of their peer coaches. Additionally, participants have cited the program as a primary impetus for their decisions to continue into a second and third year in the profession.

—*prepared by Victoria L. Bernhardt and Margaret Triplett*

Induction for the Beginning Teacher Program Staff

Director	Victoria L. Bernhardt
Instructor/Trainer	Geraldine Flaherty
Field Supervisor	Fran Rebello
Program Assistant	Margaret Triplett
Administrative Assistant	Joyce Anderson
Program Assistant	Georganne Donaldson

Contact Person:
Dr. Victoria L. Bernhardt
Induction for the Beginning Teacher Program
Director
College of Education
California State University, Chico
Chico, California 95929-0224
(916) 895-6165

SANTA CLARA NEW TEACHER PROJECT A DISTRICT PROGRAM FOR NEW TEACHER SUPPORT

The Santa Clara New Teacher Project includes kindergarten through sixth grade teachers in a unified K-12 school district. The mainly suburban district is socio-economically diverse, and the student population is nearly 50 percent non-white.

The purpose of our project was to develop an exemplary model for supporting and assessing new teachers which would result in improved learning opportunities for all students in Santa Clara Unified School District. We developed our model with the support of the local Teachers' Association, United Teachers of Santa Clara.

Our goals included providing an organizational environment where new teachers would sense support, personal success, stability and continuous professional development while undergoing transition to a new teaching job. A survey of new teachers from the previous spring showed a need for training in time management and class management.

In the first year of the project, 15 teachers participated. Nine were fresh out of teacher training; the other six were in their second year of teaching. In deciding which teachers would be a part of the project, we looked at which schools had the greatest number of new teachers. We also looked for those schools that had principals who would be very supportive, and we wanted principals who were involved in the Bay Area Administrative Training Program.

Project teachers attended a seminar series of about 15 sessions that covered all aspects of time and class management. Some of the support teachers also attended. The new teachers also attended workshops in cooperative learning strategies. The seminar meetings quickly became a time for sharing and solving common problems, and participants developed a close camaraderie. The director also used these meetings to share information about the project. At the end of the year the teachers commented on the close relationships they had developed with the seminar instructor, the director, and each other.

We wanted the new teachers to experience support from as many different people as possible. Each teacher was assigned to a mentor teacher who taught at the same grade level but usually not at the same school. Each project teacher was also linked up with a support teacher at the same grade level and school site. The on-site support person was the everyday contact with the new teacher — helping with day to day planning, answering questions, offering advice.

The project director – a middle school teacher – was released from teaching in the afternoon to manage the project. He visited the project teachers in their schools many times throughout the year, making himself available as another support person.

We also provided some incentives for people involved in the project. The new teachers received a stipend of $16 per hour for attending meetings. They also received credit toward their professional growth requirements. The on-site support teachers received $300 for the year plus the hourly stipend for attending meetings. The mentor teachers were compensated from the California Mentor Teacher Program.

For the second year of the project, the program for first year teachers is similar to that of the first year. We have added a component for the teachers who are in the project for the second year. Second year project teachers will continue working on planning and classroom management. They will also be trained to use Integrated Thematic Instruction. Mentors will take on more of a coaching role, and there will be training in collegial coaching.

Teachers who participated in the New Teacher Project last year report that beginning school this year was comparatively easy, thanks in large part to what they learned in the project last year.

—Prepared by Jim Mitchell

Santa Clara New Teacher Project Staff

Project Director   Delberta Meyer
Project Coordinator   Jim Mitchell
Project Secretary   Cathy Van Pernis

Contact Person:
Jim Mitchell
Santa Clara New Teacher Project
Santa Clara Unified School District
1889 Lawrence Road
Santa Clara, California 95052
(408) 720-8540

THE SANTA CRUZ COUNTY NEW TEACHER PROJECT

Anyone who has been a teacher remembers his or her first year of teaching — and all too often would prefer to forget it. Typically, it is an isolating, grueling, and difficult introduction to the profession. The new teacher's idealism and excitement are quickly eroded by the stress and anxiety of keeping a class "together," mastering classroom skills, and becoming a successful professional.

In Santa Cruz County Schools, the new teacher's year begins differently from most others. Forty-two first-year elementary teachers, 28 of whom are bilingual, are at the hub of an exciting collaborative effort between the university, the county office of education, and school districts to ease the transition from student teacher to experienced teacher. The Santa Cruz County New Teacher Project supports beginning teachers' efforts to translate what they have learned in preservice courses into classroom practice.

Though their task is still not easy, new teachers receive a gentler, smoother, and more supportive transition into the profession.

The project is a collaborative effort between the University of California at Santa Cruz Teacher Education Program, the Santa Cruz County Office of Education, and seven school districts in Santa Cruz County. This county-wide consortium, led by the university, is composed of 17 representatives from each sponsoring organization, including assistant superintendents, principals, personnel directors and staff development coordinators, mentor teachers, union representatives, university faculty and project staff. A distinctive feature of this project comes from the close ties developed between the university Teacher Education Program and the school districts in the area. The consortium builds on a ten-year legacy of effective collaboration between the university and county schools. The project is led by Ellen Moir, Coordinator of the Student Teaching Program at the University of California at Santa Cruz, who also serves as chair of the consortium. The consortium meets six times during the year. Consortium input directs the project and provides a unique forum unprecedented in Santa Cruz county. It facilitates communication and collaboration across districts and institutional boundaries for the purpose of supporting and assisting new teachers.

The project serves seven school districts in Santa Cruz County. Santa Cruz County is a rapidly growing area with a diverse population of about 220,000. Employment in the county is primarily in agriculture and tourism, although in recent years the computer industry has grown significantly. The seven school districts serve the needs of approximately 33,000 K-12 students.

The county's population is technically and linguistically diverse. For example, in Pajaro Valley Unified School District, the largest of the county's school districts, 40 percent of the students are Limited English Proficient, making the district one of the most linguistically impacted in the state. Ninety-four percent of these students are Spanish-speaking, and of this population, 77 percent are migrant workers. Consequently, the district is and will continue to be hiring many first-year bilingual teachers who, in addition to their special language training needs, will have to deal with the social, emotional, and academic needs of this fluctuating student population.

The Santa Cruz County New Teacher Project, one of 15 pilot projects in the state, is built upon the existing supervisory model used in the Teacher Education Program at UCSC, where exemplary local classroom teachers are hired on a rotational basis to supervise student teachers and teach methods courses. Student teachers are observed on a weekly basis for twenty weeks. This close working relationship provides a rich supportive feedback system as well as the many benefits of working with the best teachers in our local area. Four exemplary teachers — novice teacher advisors — are the cornerstone of the Santa Cruz County New Teacher Project. The advisors, two of whom specialize in bilingual education, are hired to work with novice teachers for the entire year under the guidance of a UCSC project director.

The Project's First Year

Below are some of the unique features of this project from its first year of operation:

Novice Teacher Advisors. Key to the Santa Cruz project's approach is the strong belief that the new teacher will benefit most from ongoing coaching and support with a clear understanding of what constitutes effective teacher performance in his/her particular setting.

Four advisors were hired in August, 1988 from Santa Cruz County school districts. Two bilingual advisors, one full-time and one half-time, worked with 23 bilingual first-year teachers from the Pajaro Valley Unified School District, the largest in the county. One advisor worked half-time with the Santa Cruz City School District. The other full-time advisor worked with the remaining five school districts. All of the advisors were on loan to the project while remaining as district employees. The districts were reimbursed for their entire salary and benefit package in June. Advisors worked with each new teacher on the average of two hours a week. New teachers had the opportunity to schedule the advisors' visits to be held before school, after school, or during class time. This scheduling enabled the advisors to work with each new teacher both in and out of the classroom. The advisors' time in the class was spent doing demonstration lessons, observing and coaching, team teaching, assessing students, videotaping lessons, providing release time, responding to interactive journals, and assisting with problems as they arose. Time outside was spent on planning, gathering and providing resources, problem-solving and reflection, and general support and encouragement. By being familiar with the students in the class, the overall curriculum plan, and the class structure and organization, the advisor was able to provide new teachers with specific, pertinent, concrete praise and suggestions.

As a result of the intensive involvement, each advisor developed a unique and powerful collegial relationship with each new teacher. Evaluations from the new teachers in May used such descriptors as "saint," "guardian angel," "friend," and "co-teacher" to describe this relationship. The advisor/novice partnership truly proved to be the cornerstone of the project.

One of the unanticipated benefits to new teachers was the spillover effect of the collegiality being modeled by the new teacher and the new teacher advisor. Veteran teachers at the school sites often approached new teachers or their advisors to be a part of their sharing or to receive copies of resources the advisors brought. This gave new teachers a boost in self-esteem as they could now be givers rather than always "takers."

In reflecting upon their role, advisors felt that they needed additional training in counseling skills, developing a repertoire of skills to work with the most needy new teachers, and a structure to develop their own collegiality and networking.

Individual Novice Plan. The project recognized that new teachers enter the profession at different developmental stages and with individual needs. In a non-evaluative and supportive manner, the novice teacher advisors helped each new teacher develop an individualized plan to address his/her goals and needs specifically. From week to week the advisor and the new teacher worked together as partners to strengthen the new teacher's program.

The project staff developed a Novice Teacher Log which was used to keep records of the type of contact each new teacher had on a weekly basis and to document follow-up comments on what would happen next. Close contact with principals and on-site support teachers also focused the direction of the assistance to the new teacher. In January, project staff also developed a New Teacher Self Assessment designed to have each new teacher reflect on his/her strengths and weaknesses. This self assessment serves

to focus the content of the new teacher/advisor contact during the subsequent visitations. In May and June advisors met with new teachers for a half day of reflection, curriculum development and planning for the following year.

The Individual Novice Plan was an evolving aspect of the project. As the new teacher developed through the phases of first year teaching, so did the Plan. At the beginning of the year, each week provided a new challenge for the new teacher and the advisor responded to the concern of the moment. By June, many new teachers were able to accomplish the goal of constructing a year plan for the following year, including plans for specific areas of strength and weakness identified through ongoing self-assessment and reflection. Because project staff were so closely involved with the new teachers, each plan was unique and matched the goals of each individual teacher.

On-Site Support Teacher/Buddy. New teachers were paired with an experienced teacher at their school site. Efforts were made to pair teachers of the same grade level. At an orientation meeting in September, buddies were asked to maintain regular contact with the new teachers and were given a packet explaining the project and examples of areas of support. They were also asked to keep a log of the type of service they provided the new teacher. These were collected and reviewed by project staff. Each buddy received a stipend of $225 at the end of the year.

Project staff felt that the on-site support teacher component of the project was about 50 percent effective. Some buddies were very involved and were crucial to the success of the new teacher. The other half were helpful at the beginning of the year, but assistance decreased significantly as the year progressed.

University Aides. A new course was developed at the University of California at Santa Cruz that strengthened the student teacher program (in drawing minority students and providing additional field placement opportunities) and assisted first-year teachers. University students were trained specifically to work with new teachers in their classrooms for 10 to 12 hours per week for a 10-week period. A university faculty member (another veteran teacher from a local school district) taught the class and supervised the university aides. Fifteen aides were placed in new teachers' classrooms.

Staff Development. Staff development has been a coordinated effort by the New Teacher Project staff and local districts. Each district offered a preservice orientation for its new teachers. The director and an advisor attended each orientation to introduce the New Teacher Project as well as to become familiar with each district's services to new teachers.

A key philosophy and strength of the Santa Cruz County Project was the emphasis on keeping the new teacher in the classroom, thereby limiting outside staff development activities which might detract from the teacher's growing abilities to absorb and apply material directly to his or her own class. New teachers were encouraged to become active participants in their own professional development. The project staff planned and delivered three in-service days aimed at meeting the identified needs of the new teacher. The inservices were: Classroom Management, Language Development (specifically aimed at working with language minority students), and The Reading/Writing Connection. Evaluations of these days were overwhelmingly positive. New teachers felt that they had received information which was immediately applicable and manageable within their first-year context. In addition, each new teacher planned two self-selected release days from January to June. Many worked on long-term planning with their advisor. Others observed exemplary teachers with their advisor and collaboratively discussed what they had seen to promote an application of what had been learned in terms the new teacher could use and apply.

A series of 10 seminars was offered to new teachers. The seminars provided a forum for follow-up to the inservice days as well as other topics such as classroom management, classroom organization, end-of-school procedures, stress reduction, time management, and networking among the new teachers themselves. Participants received five units of university credit. New teachers were unanimous in wanting this to continue into their second year.

Newsletter. Project staff created an informational and promotional newsletter that was distributed to all participants, on-site support teachers, principals, district administrators, and Consortium members three times during the year.

Educational Community Awareness and Networking. The project hosted a reception for the edu-

cational community in September. One hundred twenty-five educators from around the county attended, including seven superintendents, union representatives, on-site support teachers, principals, University of California at Santa Cruz faculty, new teachers, and project staff. In June, the University Chancellor hosted an end-of-the-year reception to celebrate the successful retention of 42 new teachers in the county; public school administrators, new teachers, veteran teachers, and university faculty also attended.

The Consortium assisted project staff in hosting a Symposium for educators in June. The Symposium presented the successful elements of the project. Presenters represented the project staff as well as district-level administrators, principals, the University of California at Santa Cruz Board of Studies in Education, and new teachers. The participants stated that the information presented will change and strengthen the ways in which they deal with new teachers in the future. Many asked for copies of our findings, our self-assessment instrument used to develop the Individual Novice Plan, and our chart of the phases of teaching through which a new teacher passes in a first year.

Hotline. Each advisor was available on an on-call basis for immediate support. Advisor logs indicate that an average of two to three hours a week were spent on the phone for after-hours support.

Summary

The results of this project have been far-reaching. The project has been based on a model that releases exemplary teachers from full-time classroom positions in order to form partnerships with new teachers. The strength of the project has been this intensive, individual involvement with each new teacher which provided non-judgmental, regular and sustained support over the year. An additional strength has been the collaborative nature of the project, enabling genuine teamwork, communication, and reflection within and among the participating institutions (the University of California at Santa Cruz, school district administrations, and teaching staff). For the Santa Cruz Teacher Education Program, this collaboration has provided rich feedback about how our preservice preparation works or doesn't work when tested within the reality of first year teaching; we have already begun to integrate this knowledge into our teacher preparation course-work. Twenty-six of the 42 new teachers are graduates of the university preparation program. Since the inception of the New Teacher Project, we have been able for the first time to conduct a level of graduate follow-up and support that begins to resemble the close supervision and support model to which they became accustomed during student teaching.

As a collaborative effort of the Consortium, the University of California at Santa Cruz, local districts, administrators, veteran teachers, and unions, the Santa Cruz County New Teacher Project was clearly successful in empowering and retaining 42 of tomorrow's educators.

— Prepared by Ellen Moir and Judy Stobbe

Santa Cruz New Teacher Project Staff

Project Director   Ellen Moir

Novice Teacher Advisors   Wendy Baron
                                Janette Miller
                                Carrol Moran
                                Judy Stobbe

Contact Person:
Ellen Moir
Santa Cruz County New Teacher Project
Office of Teacher Education
University of California at Santa Cruz
Santa Cruz, California 95064
(408) 429-4025

PROJECT TAP (TEACHER ASSISTANCE PROGRAM) A DISTRICT/UNIVERSITY COLLABORATIVE MODEL OF INDUCTION

Project TAP (Teacher Assistance Program), a three-phase induction model, is a collaborative project between Cajon Valley Union School District and San Diego State University. *Phase I* involves the assignment of school site start-up partners who assist new teachers in their first eight weeks of teaching. *Phase II* includes the selection of school site support team members. Teams, led by the principal, focus on assisting new teachers in areas of improving instructional performance, reflective problem-solving, and professional growth planning. *Phase III* integrates district and university educational resources at the Model Education Center, a professional develop-

ment school, in order to promote the professional growth of new teachers.

The project staff includes the school district's Assistant Superintendent for Instructional Services and a university professor who serve as Co-Directors; a teacher on special assignment who coordinates the program; the university instructional team leader of the Model Education Center who serves as a consultant; and a full-time project secretary. The staff meets with an advisory board of district and university personnel which includes the district's Superintendent of Schools and the dean of the College of Education as well as principals, mentor teachers, and teacher union representatives. In the initial year of implementation (1988-89), Project TAP served 45 first-year teachers representing 16 schools.

Phase I

As part of the hiring process, the principal at each site is responsible for assigning a start-up partner for each beginning teacher. The partner, who receives a stipend of $200 during Phase I, is expected to reflect the following characteristics:

- Be expert in creating a learning environment (a role model)

- Teach at the same grade level as the new teacher

- Be approachable and supportive

- Be experienced (have materials and ideas to share)

The roles and responsibilities of start-up partners are to:

- Welcome and orient the new teacher to the school site

- Attend Project TAP inservices for veteran educators

- Assist new teachers in beginning the school year (i.e., welcoming, assisting in securing appropriate materials, creating a learning environment, establishing a discipline plan, unit/lesson planning, assessing learning skills of students, answering questions)

- Assist new teachers in spending a $200 classroom set-up stipend (i.e., going shopping together). Stipends are spent on nonconsumable items which enhance the new teacher's classroom. These become the personal property of the new teacher.

- Participate in the evaluation of the project

The content of assistance is targeted toward areas of concern associated with beginning the school year and is individualized based on the needs of the new teacher and the contextual setting. Partners are provided with resources such as "Beginning the School Year, Pamphlet A" of Randall Sprick's *The Solution Book*, *A First Year Teacher's Guide to Success* by Bonnie Williamson, and the district new teacher handbook. Although most assistance is provided after school, the project provides release days (a half day for the novice teacher and a full day for the veteran teacher during Phase I) in order to facilitate interaction and support. In addition to assistance provided by start-up partners and the project teacher on special assignment, new teachers participate in a seminar on classroom management prior to the beginning of school, and monthly TAP RAP sessions which address topics like parent conferences, preparing for substitutes, record keeping, and testing. These meetings are led by district new teacher mentors and extend throughout the school year.

Phase II

The process of setting up the Phase II support teams involves having the principal consult with the new teachers and their partners to discuss possible reassignment of support personnel. Start-up partners are assigned to the support team if the partner match has been successful, Phase I has been implemented, and the experienced teacher is able to make the necessary time commitment given other responsibilities. This commitment includes six team meetings and three training seminars. Team members receive a $200 stipend for assisting new teachers during Phase II, which extends for approximately six months.

The focus of assistance in Phase II shifts from start-up needs to improving instructional performance, reflective problem-solving, and professional growth planning. Support team members attend two day-long seminars on reflective supervision and al-

ternative observation strategies, and an after-school seminar on developing professional growth plans. Two release days are provided for the experienced teacher and one release day is provided for the novice teacher in order to facilitate assistance during this phase. As experienced teachers work together with new teachers during this phase, assistance is given in targeting growth areas which translate into goals for a professional growth plan. As part of the plan, activities to achieve the goals are identified and recorded. The project staff plans Phase III inservice opportunities in response to these identified goals.

To promote reflective problem solving, teams engage in writing critical incident summaries at their meetings. This involves a ten minute quick-write in which the new teachers describe an incident that has been positively or negatively significant to them in their teaching. New teachers share the incidents with the group. The principal and experienced teachers serve as facilitators in the ensuing discussion as team members interact to gain insights and ideas. The goal of the discussion is to encourage new teachers to review and reflect on their own experiences as well as speculate on possible solutions to identified problems. Experienced educators are encouraged to guide new teachers in self-analysis and reflection rather than simply prescribe pat answers.

The roles and responsibilities of support team members are to:

- Attend Project TAP inservice seminars

- Organize classroom observation and conference opportunities for new teachers and experienced teachers at the school site

- Collaboratively assess new teacher strengths and target growth areas

- Assist new teachers in developing a professional growth plan

- Engage in reflective problem-solving by writing critical incident summaries and discussing particular concerns at team meetings

- Participate in the evaluation of Project TAP

Phase III

Each new teacher is provided with two release days during Phase III in which they can visit the Model Education Center and a district mentor's classroom. A wide range of inservice opportunities are developed in order to respond to the diversity of growth goals that new teachers identify in their professional growth plans. San Diego State University professors offer seminars on such topics as integrating language arts and social studies, discovery learning in science, math manipulatives, and teaching culturally diverse students. Model Education Center teachers give demonstration lessons in all subject areas at the various grade levels and conduct pre- and post-conferences with the new teachers. Strategy packets of materials are prepared to assist new teachers in implementing what they observe and learn. University and Model Education Center teachers receive a $200 stipend for participating in Phase III, which occurs during March and April.

The project teacher on special assignment is critically important to the continuity and success of Project TAP. Responsibilities include:

- Coordination, guidance and monitoring of each phase of the project in consultation with project staff, new teachers, site administrators, and assisting teachers

- Conducting informal observations of new teachers (formal observations on request)

- Participating in TAP RAP sessions for new teachers

- Supervising work of the project secretary

- Serving as a resource for lesson demonstrations

- Serving as an advocate for new teachers

- Assisting in designing and presenting seminars

- Participating in the evaluation of the project

Project Rationale

The purpose of Project TAP is to provide assis-tance in promoting the professional growth of novice teachers in the Cajon Valley Union School District and to serve as a pilot program in a statewide evaluation study on alternative models of induction for new teachers. This purpose is accomplished by: 1) individualizing assistance based on the personal and contextual needs of each new teacher; 2) providing a forum for new and experienced teachers to engage in reflective problem solving; 3) incorporating structures to ensure an effective new/experienced teacher match; 4) educating veteran educators in strategies of support and assistance; and 5) integrating district and university resources for induction.

Complexity invariably characterizes each teaching experience. Among other factors, diversity in teacher personality, prior experience, grade/class assignment, and school context interact to identify the challenge the first-year teacher encounters. Some induction programs seek to respond to this challenge by placing major emphasis on new teacher seminars in which generic content is presented. This alternative model chooses to focus educational time, energy, and resources on preparing veteran educators to assist new teachers at the school site during the initial two-thirds of the school year before offering additional opportunities for professional growth at the Model Education Center. Throughout the program, the focus is placed on addressing the individual growth needs of each new teacher.

Promoting the reflective problem-solving skills of both the veteran educator and the new teacher in relation to the specific diversity of each new teacher's setting is an additional focus of the program. Structures such as school site team meetings, critical incident summaries, and reflective supervision are all related to this objective. For many new teacher participants in the project, this is an extension of pre-service preparation. Project TAP builds on the reflective supervision training provided by the Partners in Supervision Project, a CSU clinical supervision model program at San Diego State University.

Project TAP also maximizes the assistance process by providing new and veteran teachers with the opportunity to have input in the selection of support personnel. According to Huling-Austin, Putman & Galvez-Hjornevik (1985), "The assignment of an appropriate support teacher is likely to be the most powerful and cost-effective intervention in an induction program." Achieving an effective mentor/new teacher match is complicated by the fact that support is critical at the beginning of the school year.

Unfortunately, assignments must be made before novice and veteran teachers have had an opportunity to identify how well they work together. Project TAP is designed both to ensure start-up assistance by assigning start-up partners and provide for an opportunity to change support personnel at the end of Phase I. The phase-in approach offers opportunities for interaction and rapport building to occur prior to the selection of the support teams that extend start-up assistance into a program for professional growth. All the participants of Phase I consult with the principal individually before the support team is officially assigned. Changes in support personnel can be made prior to beginning Phase II.

An assumption of this model of induction, which emphasizes preparing veteran teachers to assist new teachers, is that veteran teachers, carefully selected for their contextual understanding and content expertise, will know what a new teacher needs to learn; but they may need assistance in articulating and relating their knowledge and expertise. In addition, the experienced teacher may need to learn how to guide the new teacher in reflection rather than simply offer solutions that have worked in other settings. Seminar sessions stress how to integrate the veteran teacher's "wisdom of practice" (Shulman, 1986) with the knowledge of new teachers through content coaching in complex settings and reflective problem solving.

Modifications Based on Lessons Learned

Phase I (start-up assistance) and Phase III (integration of district/university resources for professional growth) at the Model Education Center were implemented with relative ease in the initial year of the project. In Phase I, providing one-to-one assistance at the school site was clearly understood as a valuable innovation. Participation in the partner arrangement was affirming, both to the novice and the experienced educator who was selected to assist. Principals made the assignments efficiently and effectively. Phase III involved utilizing teaching teams at the Model Education Center who were already actively interacting as part of an ongoing staff development plan. The tasks of preparing strategy packets and providing demonstration lessons for novice teachers were new but the structures for accomplishing the

tasks (i.e., cross-grade team planning) were in place. The Model Education Center has been a collaborative district/university program since 1986. In contrast, Phase II (support team assistance) involved creating new expectations and new structures for realizing those expectations. Evaluation data indicated that this phase was particularly significant for new teachers in schools where principals identified with the recommended theory and practice of Phase II and assumed active leadership in implementing this phase. However, several teams did not meet consistently. In the second year of implementation, intensive effort is being made to help each school site principal and support team clarify the goals and structures associated with Phase II. In addition to veteran educator seminars, project staff representatives will be attending each team's initial meeting to model a reflective approach to problem solving, and to help clarify expectations associated with classroom observations and targeting professional growth goals.

All innovations require time and effort to move from implementation to institutionalization. Fortunately, the district and university have evidenced a high level of enthusiasm and commitment to the goal of assisting new teachers through this model of induction.

— Prepared by Diane S. Murphy

Project TAP
Teacher Assistance Program Staff

District Co-Director	Yvonne Johnson
University Co-Director	Diane S. Murphy
Project Teacher on Special Assignment	Chris Keitel
University Consultant	Marlowe Berg
Secretary	Mary Cooper

Contact Person:
Dr. Diane S. Murphy
Project TAP
Cajon Valley Union School District
189 Roanoke Road, P.O. Box 1007
El Cajon, California. 92022
(619) 588-3002

CHAPTER 8

A Policy Framework for New Teacher Support

Douglas E. Mitchell
David Hough
University of California, Riverside

EFFECTIVE teaching, like quality work in any other occupation, does not just happen. Good teaching begins with the motivation of able young people to obtain appropriate training and seek employment in the public schools. Motivation alone is not enough, of course. Creating high quality teacher training programs, carefully screening graduates before hiring, and insuring that, once hired, teachers are given a supportive environment and held accountable for their assigned tasks, are all critical ingredients in a high performance school system. Faced with complexities such as these, policy makers usually ask, "What are the most important points of leverage?" In other words, what are the most cost-effective means for improving the system?

This chapter is devoted to wrestling with this basic policy question. We begin by taking the broadest possible look at the labor market processes shaping overall teacher recruitment, training, employment, and supervision in the schools. Within the framework of this labor market system, we then look closely at the state-supported new teacher support programs, examining what role they can be expected to play in shaping the effectiveness of California's nearly 200,000 public school teachers. Two dimensions of these programs will be examined: 1) the nature of the services they should be expected to provide, and 2) the distribution of authority and responsibility for insuring the proper induction of new teachers into the complexities and subtleties of high quality teaching.

THE POLICY PROBLEM: A LABOR MARKET FOCUS

Public policy decisions always involve a balancing act. Since problems are numerous and resources always limited, policy makers must decide **which** problems should be addressed, and **how much** money, regulatory attention, or programmatic support should be allocated to ameliorating them. Even before a problem can be attacked, it must be conceptualized in a way that allows policy makers to imagine taking constructive action. Problems that are attributed to fate, or the exercise of personal liberties, or that are producing no demand for solutions are simply ignored by the policy system. Conversely, problems that have mobilized powerful interest groups are seen as either the "proper business of government" or the cause of social unrest and criminal activity, and those get high priority.

Schools and school improvement are no exceptions. Americans have a century-long tradition of public support for free, compulsory education of all children. As David Easton (1965) noted in his classic formulation of the political process, this tradition involves both demand and support — demand for schooling that prepares children for success in the adult world, and support in the form of huge budgets and broad legal authority for teachers and administrators. Over the years, attention by both citizens and political leaders has oscillated between an emphasis on *demanding better schools* and *supporting educators* in their attempts to produce them. During periods when demand is high and support relatively weak, policy makers emphasize raising requirements, elaborating assessment, and strengthening accountability for

performance. When the pendulum swings in the other direction and support considerations become prominent, policy makers tend to debate increased school funding and the development of new and innovative programs to enhance the work of professional educators.

The 1980s have witnessed a unique mixture of intense and rapidly shifting policy demands and supports for the public schools. Early in the decade the shrill rhetoric of the National Commission on Excellence (1983) report, *A Nation at Risk*, unleashed an avalanche of demand-oriented reform proposals. Schools were seen as mired in "mediocrity," seriously undermining the nation's security by failing to prepare students for productivity in a global economy. As the decade comes to a close, however, support-oriented policies have begun to surface once again. Today's policy makers recognize that reform and improvement require the dedicated effort and enthusiastic engagement of professional educators — not just the adoption of standards and mandates for accountability. Thus, proper funding of public schooling, symbolized in the passage of Proposition 98, innovative programs, and the development of curriculum materials, training of managers, and numerous other aspects of school operations are receiving widespread interest and support.

The state-supported California New Teacher Project and the Inner City New Teacher Retention Project are among the more imaginative and potentially far-reaching of these new school support policies. These aim at school improvement by facilitating entry into the occupation for new teachers who might otherwise be consumed in the "baptism by fire" that awaits newly certified teachers as they enter the public schools. The new teacher programs were developed in response to a growing awareness that college- and university-based training programs cannot adequately prepare teachers for the rigors and tensions that accompany the first year or two of classroom work. Too many young teachers fall by the wayside during their first years on the job — victims of disillusionment, alienation, and stress.

Can the California new teacher programs provide the needed transition from preservice training and certification to full-time classroom responsibility? If they can, are these programs more cost-effective than reduced teaching work loads, a longer training period, recruitment of more able or more

FIGURE 1
LABOR MARKET DEVELOPMENT STRATEGIES

Labor Market Improvement Strategies	Labor Market Membership	Policy Magnets	Policy Screens	Direct Fiscal	Indirect Fiscal
1. Motivate	Eligibles	Publicize	Disclose	Base Salary	School Funding
2. Train	Talented	Innovate	Requirements	Offset Training Costs	Program Development
3. Select	Qualified	Recruit	Assess	Placement Systems Development	Differentiated Staffing
4. Induct	Enlisted	Support	Counsel	Support Services	Release Time
5. Develop	Successful	Reward	Evaluate	Career Ladders	Professionalize Teaching

mature teacher candidates, or any other strategies for increasing the probability of bringing highly qualified and dedicated long-term teachers into the work force? One starting point for answering these questions is to look at the overall labor market for teachers — from motivation and training through recruitment, selection, induction, and ongoing support.

THE PLACE OF SUPPORT PROGRAMS IN THE TEACHER LABOR MARKET

Induction programs like those supported by the California New Teacher Project and the California New Teacher Retention Project play an important role in facilitating high job performance in any occupation. Many employers use some form of orientation or apprenticeship program to help new workers learn specific job requirements or adjust to the work environment. Long-term induction programs may take several years and involve complex learning processes — as required of medical interns or law clerks, for example. In most jobs the induction process is much shorter, lasting from a few minutes to several weeks as new workers learn overall job requirements, demonstrate competencies, or merely practice under close supervision.

As indicated in Figure 1, however, induction programs are but a small part of the overall labor market picture. Long before induction programs can be used, employees have to be motivated to enter an occupation. Those motivated have to acquire needed

experience and training to qualify for employment, and qualified workers have to be selected for employment. Only then can effective induction programs be used to provide the skills, social relationships, and workplace orientation needed for successful job performance.

As indicated in the first column of Figure 1, policy makers have five distinct labor market improvement strategies available to them for enhancing the overall quality of school teaching. Each of these labor market improvement strategies is the subject of a large body of research and scholarly interest as well as being the object of ongoing education policy debates. In the paragraphs that follow, we briefly review each of the five labor market enhancement strategies in order to identify the place of induction support programs within an overall policy framework.

Each of the labor market enhancement strategies is described by answering five key questions:

1. What does the labor market look like from this perspective, who are the members of the pool, and how are they identified for review and support?

2. What sorts of policies could be used as "magnets" to increase the number and quality of the teaching work force at this stage?

3. What sorts of policies could be used as "screens" to reduce the likelihood that weak or low-performing teachers will enter the schools and/or continue to serve in classrooms?

4. If policy makers sought to provide direct fiscal support or incentives to strengthen the labor market at this stage, what sorts of fiscal mechanisms are available?

5. What general fiscal strategies can be used to enhance the labor market at this stage, if policy makers wish to improve the teaching work force indirectly — that is, by providing fiscal resources that local educators or other key actors may use to improve the likelihood that the teaching work force will improve?

We turn now to a review of each strategy in light of these five questions.

Motivating the Eligible

In teaching, as in any other labor market, the first problem is to find a way to motivate eligible young people to seek needed training and apply for work in the occupation. While motivation is the critical element at this point, it is important to target motivation programs on those who already are or can become eligible for employment in the field. The result of motivating ineligible people is pain and suffering, not successful employment. Just as athletic teams, performing artist groups, and highly technical occupations like engineering or medicine try to target their recruitment of new employees on individuals who have the requisite talents and interests, teaching recruitment is enhanced when motivation is appropriately targeted.

To attract eligible young teachers, schools publicize available job opportunities — emphasizing those aspects of the job that are most likely to attract individuals with needed skills and interests. While education salaries are modest, they have been moving up in recent years. Job security, the stimulation of working with children, and the satisfaction of performing a highly valued service are also attractive features of the teaching profession. Whether potential teachers are attracted by a 180-day student contact work year with six-hour student contact days or repelled by the emotional drain of this intense interpersonal contact

is not entirely certain. In any event, young people are drawn into teaching through the use of policy magnets that publicize the positive features of the work.

It has recently become evident that the publicity system works too well for some young people. A number of individuals who lack either the temperament or the talent to become good teachers have, unfortunately, entered the occupation naively unaware of its real demands. Hence, some have recommended that policy makers create more effective screening devices to discourage these teacher candidates before they take extensive training or actually seek public school employment. When dealing with the large pool of eligible workers who have yet to decide upon a teaching career, the best screening device is probably full disclosure of the emotional and intellectual rigors of this line of work. Bringing many more college students into the schools as teacher aides or student tutors would probably go a long way toward disclosing the real nature of the occupation and providing eligible students with a solid basis for deciding whether to seek preservice training.

Two types of fiscal policies are appropriate for motivating more eligible young people to seek teaching careers. Direct fiscal motivation is provided when policy makers directly fund teachers' base salaries. This approach insures that local administrators do not use these earmarked resources for capital development or other non-salary items. A less direct approach to making schools attractive to eligible young people is to simply raise overall school funding levels. Where policy makers are confident that local decision makers can strike a proper balance between salary and non-salary aspects of the program, they are well advised to simply raise overall school budgets. Local variations in the cost of various program needs and local labor market variables often make direct funding of particular program components unproductive for some schools or districts.

Incentives for future teachers that will attract the most able college students and present teaching in a favorable light foster commitment to the occupation over the long term. Especially in California, where teacher shortages and rapid turnover in staff are affecting the quality of instruction for many school children, fiscal incentives can significantly reduce the shortage of teachers. Although California will need between 15,000 and 17,000 teachers each year through the 1990s, the number of new teachers being trained in colleges and universities is on the decline (PACE, 1988). This suggests that fiscal as well as non-fiscal incentives for eligible teacher candidates need to be raised significantly.

Training the Talented

Once able young people are motivated to enter the profession, the teacher labor market enters a new phase where training rather than motivation is the primary policy consideration. Even the most highly motivated teacher candidates — those who see teaching as a rewarding occupation, find schools stimulating, and feel that classrooms are places where they gain personal worth by enriching the lives of children — cannot enter their chosen profession until they obtain adequate training.

At this point costs rise, but membership in the teacher labor market shrinks dramatically. Motivation programs must reach a very large number of potential teacher candidates. By contrast, expensive training programs can be rather narrowly focused on the much smaller number of individuals who are talented enough to be successful in the field.

Throughout the twentieth century, state policy makers have made very large investments in improving the quality and character of teacher training. Early state efforts involved development of certification standards and creation of "Normal" schools aimed at meeting these standards. Normal school programs were intended to upgrade the subject matter knowledge and pedagogical skills of the rapidly expanding teacher work force. Using relatively short training programs, these schools were designed to improve the skills of a large number of teachers who had little or no college level training. As the twentieth century progressed, training requirements were expanded. Normal schools became building blocks in the development of public colleges and universities in most states, and teacher certification became linked to completion of a baccalaureate degree. In a few states, notably California, legislators extended preservice training beyond the baccalaureate level to include postgraduate training.

In addition to the establishment of special schools and training programs, policy makers linked teacher salaries to the acquisition of increased training. Originally, the link between salary and formal training was intended to insure that all teachers would complete a Bachelor of Arts or Bachelor of Science degree. Once started, however, the salary linkage was extended to include masters' and even doctoral degrees.

In recent years teacher training programs have come under widespread attack as dull, inadequate and outdated. Two messages are at the heart of this criticism. The first, and harshest, criticisms have been directed toward the so-called "methods" courses. Critics contend that the methods taught lack a solid theoretical base, and amount to little more than "war stories" by former teachers who are often out of touch with changing student characteristics and unfamiliar with changing curricula. The second criticism focuses on the lack of subject matter expertise among teacher program graduates. An early leader in responding to this criticism, California eliminated undergraduate majors in education, mandated subject area majors for teacher candidates, and in 1968 essentially made teacher preparation into a postgraduate program.

This history of criticism and response illustrates the critical role played by policy in shaping the training phase of the teacher labor market. Policy makers have at their disposal both screening devices and candidate magnets that can be used to adjust the training process.

Primary responsibility for training future teachers has been a function of institutions of higher education with specific requirements for certification mandated (in varying forms) by the states. While individual school districts adhere to state requirements and select new teachers from the existing pool of college and university graduates, these same districts typically have little or no control over the applicant's prior training.

It is not entirely discernible whether colleges and universities are failing to train talented students in their charge, whether states are mandating requirements that fail to adequately screen new teachers, or whether districts are selecting the least, rather than the most, talented. However, when it is perceived that teacher preparation programs can be improved to provide necessary, comprehensive, and uniform training, alternative approaches emerge. Recently, schools of education have moved to embed their programs more fully into the public schools. For example, the Comprehensive Teacher Education Institutes in California seek to involve public schools more fundamentally in teacher training programs.

The fiscal policy approaches used to link teacher training with school organizational needs include: 1) offsetting training costs and 2) supporting training program development. The first provides direct fiscal support to the training of talented teacher candidates, the second enhances training indirectly by increasing the quality of available training opportunities. At present, offsetting teacher training costs through shared personnel and increased investment in teacher training programs appears to be increasing in popularity among policy makers. Again, the model provided by the Institute project may help shed some light on the efficacy of the indirect, program quality improvement strategy.

Selecting the Qualified

After prospective teachers have been motivated and trained, a selection process is used to review training quality and candidate character. Membership in the labor pool at this juncture shrinks substantially once again. In the case of teaching, the work force is restricted to those qualified to meet the needs of a particular school or district. Selection consists of two complementary processes: 1) assessing competency and fit, and 2) recruiting qualified candidates for specific jobs. Assessment processes represent policy screens; recruitment programs generate the offsetting magnets to attract quality teacher candidates.

Assessment is more difficult than it may at first appear. While teacher training programs all lead to the same formal certification, they have very different program emphases and produce teachers with widely varying skills and abilities. Moreover, individuals completing the same program benefit in widely different ways from their experiences.

Establishing an adequate fit between the skills, temperament, interests and educational philosophy of an individual teacher and the needs of a particular school or classroom is an even more difficult task. Prospective employers get too little data to competently make this important assessment of most job applicants. More important, bias and prejudice frequently replace sound judgment in these matters. While teacher candidates are legitimately screened to assure that they adhere to community moral standards and respect cultural norms and values, they cannot be expected to create cultural norms where none exist or to enforce the parochial interests and biases of special interest groups.

Often formal program requirements bear little relation to real competency. According to most state teaching requirements, for example, Walter Cronkite would not be "qualified" to teach high school journalism. He may be eligible for a special eminence credential or to serve as an adjunct professor at a college or university, but cannot be routinely certified. Many, perhaps most, university professors do not have the necessary certification to teach in the public schools throughout America.

Several states acknowledge alternative entrance mechanisms into the teaching market. One large group supports various internship programs to provide an alternative avenue to access. And many states issue emergency credentials for personnel in districts unable to secure qualified teachers. While eminence credentials and internships are innovations geared toward improvement, emergency credentials are more attuned to school needs and are often seen as an alternative to rigorous recruitment and assessment procedures associated with the more traditional entry system.

In contrast with assessment procedures, teacher recruitment programs provide the magnet side of teacher selection policy. In many labor markets substantial sums of money are spent on advertising to attract new recruits. Schools do not seem to find this to be a cost-efficient policy approach, however. Some have suggested that schools incorporate the collaborative effort among all key institutions to form partnerships designed to augment teacher recruitment programs.

When it comes to providing financial support for the selection process, policy makers can make a direct contribution by facilitating the development of more effective and more powerful teacher placement systems. A new teacher placement system pulls resources together in an effort to reach more prospective teachers by advertising positions nationally and by trying innovative approaches. One example of an innovative approach is the establishment of a bulletin board system that monitors both teaching vacancies and qualified applicants. Such a system monitors more accurately and efficiently prospective teachers, their interests, qualifications, and intentions.

A more indirect approach to financing better teacher selection lies in reducing the risks of assessment and recruitment efforts. If, for example, states create strong teacher career ladders or other forms of differentiated staffing, local districts can place teachers in the environments best suited to their particular mix of talents and interests. As job performance competencies are demonstrated, the staff members can move to positions of greater responsibility or to ones better suited to their individual traits and abilities.

Assessing the personal abilities and contributions that those selected for membership might make ultimately rests with the employing agency. No definitive guidelines that produce incontrovertible decisions have yet been devised. However, review processes often make use of differentiated staffing, a direct way to determine job placement. That is, different jobs require different skills, abilities, and personalities, and the proper job placement based upon these characteristics is the goal of most personnel departments, regardless of the labor market.

Support for New Teachers: Inducting the Enlisted

As indicated by the highlighted entries in Figure 1, new teacher support programs operate relatively late in the overall labor market structure. Only after a new teacher has been selected and hired does the question of how best to support entry into the new job become paramount. In education, as in most occupations, new staff members generally need both time and supportive assistance if they are to achieve peak performance. They almost always find themselves faced with unique problems and special building, program, or student characteristics. Hence, induction support programs can be very helpful if they provide systematic orientation to the unique expectations and conditions found in the new school or district.

Additionally, teacher training programs are rather brief, short-term experiences, compared to those in other professions. Therefore, new teachers frequently need supplementary training in specific skills and techniques for effective job performance. Induction support programs provide two additional types of skill and experience that can greatly enhance early job performance. First, induction programs can help link new teachers to a collegial support group made up of peer teachers and administrators. Second, well-supported induction programs can facili-

tate adjustment by providing new teachers with assistance in handling some tasks so that they have an opportunity to gradually assume full responsibility, rather than be plunged into the "baptism by fire" that results when they are thrown entirely onto their own resources during the first critical months of a new job.

Inducting new employees into the work place involves both formal and informal processes. Imbedded in these processes are some combination of *support* mechanisms and employee *counseling* activities. Support services serve as policy magnets — making the job transition easier and encouraging long-term commitment to teaching careers. Employee counseling services serve as screening devices to ameliorate anxiety, direct attention to improved job performance, or guide the misplaced teachers into another job. Beginning teachers who participate in induction programs are expected to gain a more accurate perspective on the complexities involved in teacher effectiveness. New teachers will either readily adapt to classroom rigors, derive satisfaction and reward as a result of performing well, and remain in the occupation; or they will come to recognize job demands incompatible with personal skills, abilities, and/or personality traits, and their dissatisfaction will induce a career change.

The focus of the state-supported new teacher programs in California is enlisting new teachers for participation in an ongoing program of support. The primary goal of this enlistment is to increase teacher effectiveness by providing one or more of the following: needed skills and knowledge, improved classroom performance, adjustment to the school social system, and determination to remain in the occupation. Individual needs determine the type of support that will be most beneficial.

The fiscal policies needed to make teacher induction successful center around direct funding to create and sustain various support services, and indirect funding for teacher release time and other workload control programs. Direct funding, like that provided to districts and universities participating in the California projects for new teachers, enables state policy makers to define the nature and extent of the support provided. Indirect funding through such mechanisms as new teacher workload reductions puts control over the content of the support program into the hands of the teachers themselves.

Developing the Successful

Concern for management of the teacher labor market does not end with successful induction. Current statistics confirm what sensitive policy makers have long known: good teachers leave the occupation too frequently while marginal teachers tend to languish and become emotionally "burned out" from stress and overwork. Hence, a fifth labor market improvement strategy — professional development for successful teachers — is an integral part of any comprehensive policy for teacher support and improvement.

At a minimum, professional development means: 1) encouraging continued expansion of teacher skills and abilities, 2) regular updating of subject and pedagogical knowledge, 3) growth in overall responsibility for school programs and operations, and 4) increasing self-awareness and enhancing the capacity for self-assessment and self-improvement.

There are at least two key elements in this professional development process. The first is the magnetic power of a reward system capable of providing teachers with both intrinsic rewards such as a sense of significance and suitable economic incentives. A second key element is the screening power of an effective evaluation system capable of holding teachers accountable without making them feel belittled or threatened. Neither of these basic professional development policies is easy to formulate or implement. Teacher salaries remain low compared to those of other professions. Moreover, the powerful intrinsic rewards provided by students to successful teachers are difficult to control through formal policy. It is also difficult to develop and implement teacher evaluation systems capable of seriously challenging low performing teachers or substantially rewarding those doing an outstanding job. The problem is partly a matter of infrequent and inadequate observation of actual teaching performances. It is exacerbated by the extent to which teaching philosophy and personal preferences seriously affect the ability of well-intentioned educators to reach consensus on the definition of quality teaching.

In recent years, stimulated in part by substantial Carnegie Foundation investments, teacher assessments have become more sophisticated, and there is a growing belief that effective teachers can be identified and appropriately rewarded.

Fiscal policies aimed at professional development for successful teachers include targeted funding for merit-based career ladder programs and broad-based support for professionalism among teachers. A substantial number of states and local districts are now experimenting with career ladder programs that include various levels of special funding. Fiscal support for professionalism includes such things as creation of teacher-controlled professional standards boards, substantial salary increases for the entire profession, and enhanced support for mentor teacher programs, inservice training, teacher aides, and other programs providing direct support to experienced teachers.

In sum, the first question facing education policy makers is whether induction programs to support new teachers are both valuable and feasible. This question is best answered through a careful analysis of teacher labor market conditions. To concentrate fiscal resources and administrative energy on the development of new teacher support programs, three propositions about current labor market conditions should be true:

1. New teachers are:

- inadequately prepared for the complexities and rigors of the job, or

- learning inappropriate and unproductive work attitudes and habits during their first few years, or

- leaving the occupation at an unacceptably high rate.

2. Problems related to induction are more serious than those involving recruitment, training, selection, or ongoing support and professional development, or

There is reason to believe that modest investment in this aspect of the labor market will make especially large improvements in the prospects of success for new teachers.

3. The format and content of effective support programs are well known and their implementation is feasible in both cost and organizational terms.

Proposition #1 is widely recognized to be true. Exit from teaching is very high during the first five years. So high, in fact, that two or more talented teacher candidates need to be trained for every full-time teaching position. If this high rate of early exit could be reduced, the resources now used for training could be concentrated on providing better quality training for the best motivated and most highly talented members of the labor pool now going through preservice training programs, or shifted to other needs.

Proposition #2 is harder to evaluate. Induction problems are serious, but so also are problems of recruitment, training, selection and professional development. Whether California policy makers should expand the two state-supported new teacher projects to provide comprehensive induction programs for all new teachers in the state depends on whether the costs of induction can be offset by savings in recruitment, training, selection, or professional development. At an annual cost ranging from $1,000 to $5,000 per teacher, the new teacher projects compare favorably with the costs for preservice training but are rather more expensive than current staff development programs. This is relatively expensive, however, when compared with current recruitment and selection policies. Thus, to be sustained, programs for new teachers should deliver substantial teacher quality improvements — improvements at least comparable to those produced by present preservice and inservice training practices.

Should policy makers consider shifting funds from preservice and inservice training to recruitment, selection and induction programs? Available data simply cannot answer this question. Recruitment is clearly an important problem, deserving more resources than are now being devoted to it. Selection improvements depend on the development of improved assessment instruments, an area of weakness that has been receiving substantial attention in recent years. Inservice programs have recently come under close scrutiny. They may be costing more than they are worth, but most policy makers seem inclined to fix the quality and content of existing inservice programs rather than shift attention to other aspects of the labor market.

Determining whether proposition #3 is true is a primary objective in both the California New Teacher Project and the New Teacher Retention Project. By

pilot testing and closely evaluating a variety of induction support programs, California policy makers can determine the most appropriate content for such programs, and can get some idea of the cost of providing various kinds of support services. Policy makers would be well advised to carefully review the findings of the Southwest Regional Educational Laboratory evaluation study of the two California projects. They might also engage in an ongoing dialogue with the projects' program managers who are accumulating invaluable personal insights into the problems and possibilities of facilitating new teacher induction into the profession.

While the data on new teacher program success are still being collected and analyzed, it is already possible to identify basic questions that need to be answered in order to understand how induction support programs contribute to teacher success. Funded new teacher programs involve a wide variety of organizational arrangements and draw upon a broad range of participation by administrators, university faculty members, and more experienced teacher colleagues for the delivery of the actual services. On two basic questions, however, the funded projects can be seen as offering distinctive patterns of support — patterns that could be tested for their relative importance in enhancing the long term motivation and performance of new teachers. These two questions are:

1. Are new teachers best served by enhancing specific pedagogical and subject matter knowledge and skills, or are they better served by early assistance in developing strong collegial and professional relationships?

2. Should induction support be linked to the specific school site or district where a new teacher works, or is it more effective to concentrate on induction programs that assist new teachers in understanding and adopting a broad-based professional role orientation?

The next section of this paper explores different ways of organizing induction support programs once these questions are answered. While our exploration of program alternatives remains theoretical and a bit abstract at this point, we look forward to reviewing the findings of the Southwest Regional Educational

FIGURE 2
INDUCTION PROGRAM ALTERNATIVES

	Site Specific Induction	Professional Role Induction
Expand Skill/Knowledge	Program Knowledge Development	Professional Standards Acquisition
Enhance Collegial Relationships	Work Group Solidarity	Professional Identity Development

Laboratory study to determine how successfully each of the pilot new teacher support projects deals with these fundamental issues.

SHAPING SUPPORT PROGRAMS TO MEET TEACHER ORIENTATION NEEDS

Figure 2 illustrates how induction program content is affected by the two questions posed above. The rows distinguish between programs emphasizing expansion of identifiable skill and knowledge from those aimed at enhancing collegial relationships. The columns separate site-specific programs from those aimed at supporting the development of broad-based professional work roles.

Large numbers of new teachers need support programs of the type shown in the upper left cell of Figure 2. These programs — let's call them *Program Knowledge Development* — involve familiarizing new teachers with the curriculum materials, management systems, and program goals that govern operations in their own local school or district. Such programs are especially attractive to policy makers and local leaders who feel that preservice teacher training programs do not prepare new teachers who have information about specific programs being used in a particular school. Equally important, the approach shown in this cell is closely aligned with what might be called the "labor" model of teaching (Mitchell & Kerchner, 1983). In this model, teaching effectiveness is assumed to spring directly from diligent and faithful implementation of district or school-adopted programs and curricula. Induction, in this model, means learning the specifics of local programs and learning to implement these program elements in one's assigned classroom.

The upper right hand cell of Figure 2 identifies induction support programs that aim at expanding the knowledge of professional standards and practices among teachers — let's call them the *Professional Standards Acquisition* support programs. As with those shown in the first cell, these programs concentrate on expanding technical knowledge and skills, but differ from the first group in adopting a much broader definition of the needed skills and abilities. In this cell are support programs that insist that teaching is a "skilled craft" rather than a laboring type of work. Support programs in this quadrant are viewed warmly by policy makers and school leaders who feel that teaching involves complex processes that are difficult to master. This view leads to the belief that preservice training is too short to be complete, and that important skills can only be learned in the classroom. Leaders who favor this approach want induction programs to help new teachers become continuous learners, constantly searching for new and better pedagogical techniques.

In the lower left cell of the figure are work group collegiality or solidarity induction programs. These programs — let's call them the *Work Group Solidarity* support programs — emphasize the importance of enhancing collegial relationships for teachers, but join the first group in emphasizing the importance of site-specific induction and support. This approach is compatible with the view that teaching is a type of "performing art" — an emotionally demanding task which requires a certain amount of talent to perform successfully. For policy makers and leaders holding this view, the local work group plays a key role in providing needed emotional support for the new teacher, support that enables the new teacher to sustain engagement in the act of teaching despite tension and uncertainty regarding how to perform well. These induction programs tend to emphasize the importance of mentoring, coaching, and peer tutoring among teachers in order to help each member of the staff tap into reserves of personal energy and strength.

In the lower right cell of Figure 2 are work group enhancement programs that emphasize membership in the broader teaching profession — let's call them the *Professional Identity Development* programs. These programs rely on development of collegial relationships to provide emotional support and guidance for new teachers, but emphasize the need for colleagues to bring a breadth of vision and dedication to standards of service and ethical conduct appropriate to a professional work role. Such induction programs are linked to the "professional" model of teaching work. In this model, teaching is a work of special responsibility understood and practiced only by thoroughly trained and dedicated individuals who resist political pressures and parochial cultural norms in order to bring their students access to the broadest possible range of human wisdom and knowledge. This approach to new teacher induction seeks to raise the standards of the entire educational system by forming a cadre of dedicated professionals who maintain shared values and a mutual support system.

These four distinctive approaches to defining the content and goals of induction support programs for new teachers lead to the creation of sharply divergent support services. Arguments over which of these services are really needed by new teachers are only partially amenable to empirical resolution. While careful research would shed considerable light on the extent to which new teachers lack knowledge of local program elements or awareness of professional standards, and would help determine whether collegial isolation or lack of technical knowledge are most troublesome, advocates of these different induction support programs can be expected to maintain support for their favorite approach on the grounds that it responds to the "real" problems faced by new teachers. These "real" problems are defined as much by one's view of the nature of good teaching as by detailed information about the problems faced by any specific group of new teachers.

This observation leads to the conclusion that policy makers need to give careful consideration to questions of control over the development and implementation of new teacher induction support programs.

Allocation of Authority and Responsibility

No discussion of policy would be complete without giving at least some attention to the issue of control. If, as our analysis indicates, the California New Teacher Projects are appropriately conceived as a labor market strategy for enhancing the development of one or more of the four distinctive teacher work orientations described above, we need to ask: Who should determine the specific nature of the support services to be provided, and who should decide which teachers to support?

It is easy enough to list the candidates for this control. They include:

1. State officials (State Department of Education or the Commission on Teacher Credentialing)

2. Intermediate agencies (County Offices of Education)

3. Local School Districts

4. School Sites

5. Individual Teachers

6. Teacher Organizations

7. Institutions of Higher Education or other public/private agencies

It is much harder, however, to know how to distribute to each of these agencies the appropriate mixture of responsibility and authority. Past experience suggests that individual teachers, left to their own devices, tend to "grin and bear it," heroically overcoming adversity or simply leaving the profession. Such conditions do not produce promising candidates for complete control over the induction process. These candidates do, however, need sufficient control over their own professional lives to prevent exploitation and abuse.

Institutions of higher education, once seen as the primary source of teacher quality improvement, have been criticized in recent years. While these institutions have moved to respond, their authority may be limited in years to come. At the same time, we should note that public investment in higher education is very substantial and that these agencies need to be given responsibilities commensurate with their resources.

The analysis of capacity for teacher support and of the inclination of various agencies to turn that capacity into high quality direct services needs to be applied to each of the seven key players. Where that analysis would take us depends, however, on another critical element that needs to be developed before further analysis of each key group's resources and predilections will be helpful. That key element is the choice made among the four different types of support outlined in the preceding section of this chapter (i.e., local program knowledge, professional practice knowledge, peer relationship development, or professional identity formation).

Where new teacher needs include acquisition of local program knowledge and skills, individual teachers and site level leaders can be expected to make appropriate decisions. If, however, the primary need for new skill and knowledge is more professional in character, agencies more remote from the classroom are more likely to provide appropriate leadership.

By the same token, if local level collegiality is the dominant need, teacher organizations are good candidates for control. Intermediate agencies and higher education institutions are better candidates if broad-based professional collegiality is the crucial need.

In short, while control over teacher support programs is a fundamental question in any policy analysis, answers to that question will remain speculative and tentative until questions about the content of needed programs are settled, and the relative importance of induction support for new teachers is established in relation to other labor market interventions.

CONCLUSION: A POLICY FRAMEWORK FOR NEW TEACHER SUPPORT

Elements that frame the policies adopted to institutionalize new teacher support programs fall into three categories: 1) the components of a teaching labor market, 2) induction alternatives that can be viewed as job orientations, and 3) control, delineated contextually as responsibility and authority. Each plays an essential role in framing new teacher induction/support policy.

Although induction is a *bona fide* labor market improvement strategy, it is but one facet among the variety of options. Decisionmakers will sort through these available options and determine where to concentrate time, money, and energy, and in what amounts. If, indeed, it is determined that *induction* is either most lacking among the labor market improvement strategies or is the most effective and efficient option, then policy can focus more narrowly in this direction.

Once induction is targeted for improvement, four alternatives rooted in the job orientations of labor, craft, art, and profession can be analyzed. Whether skills and knowledge or collegial relationships command more attention, and whether the primary focus is directed locally at the school site or more generally to the profession *in toto* will dictate the direction support policy takes.

Finally, the decision about where ultimate control of support programs rests belongs in the hands of the seven key groups who share individually and collectively varying degrees of responsibility and authority. A complicated mix of issues can thus be sorted, analyzed, and scrutinized as new teacher program evaluations produce data from which policy decisions will be made.

REFERENCES

Easton, D. (1965). *A systems analysis of political life.* New York: John Wiley.

Mitchell, D.E. & Kerchner, C.T. (1983). Labor relations and teacher policy. In L. Shulman and G. Sykes (Eds.), *Handbook of teaching and policy* (pp.214-238). New York: Longman.

National Commission on Excellence in Education. (1983). *A nation at risk: The imperative for educational reform.* Washington, DC: GPO.

Policy Analysis for California Education. (1988). *Conditions of education in California.* Berkeley, CA: Author.

CHAPTER 9

Beginning Teacher Assessment Activities and Developments in California*

Gary D. Estes
Kendyll Stansbury
Claudia Long
Far West Laboratory

THROUGHOUT the nation there is renewed interest in and commitment to educational excellence. We have seen many recent analyses of American education (Boyer, 1983; Goodlad, 1984; President's Commission for Excellence in Education, 1983) and proposals for its reform (Holmes Group, 1986; Shulman and Sykes, 1986; Carnegie Corporation, 1986). Although numerous different aspects of the educational enterprise have received attention and suggestions for improvement, there has been particular emphasis on the preparation, credentialing, and support of new teachers.

This paper is based upon work performed pursuant to Contract TCC-9023 with the California Interagency Task Force of the California Commission on Teacher Credentialing and the California State Department of Education New Teacher Project. The contents do not necessarily reflect the views or policies of these agencies and the accuracy of the information is the sole responsibility of the authors.

Discussion has also centered on the further development of teaching as a profession, principally through an increased emphasis on quality control over personnel, opportunities for professional development, and expansion of career roles for classroom teachers (e.g., Wise and Darling-Hammond, 1987; Shulman and Sykes, 1986).

The new emphases on beginning teacher preparation and support and on the development of teaching as a profession, are moving states toward candidate- rather than program-based modes of assessment. To enhance the caliber of teacher candidates, there is a trend toward setting higher standards for teacher preparation programs, e.g., toughening requirements for program entry and matriculation and/or more clearly specifying competencies to be mastered. States are also adopting new assessments, and prospective teachers must pass these exams to be credentialed.

Like other states, California is particularly concerned with maximizing the quality of teaching in its schools. The state has moved to evaluate individual teachers by using instruments that purport to assess teacher competence: California Basic Educational Skills Test (CBEST), the National Teachers Exam (NTE) Core Battery, and the NTE Specialty Area Tests. In recent years, these tests have been reviewed by California teachers and teacher educators for their appropriateness in the credentialing process (Wheeler and Elias, 1983; Wheeler, 1988).

The 1987-1988 review of 15 NTE Specialty Area Tests by over 400 California educators raised some major issues. The primary concern reported by reviewers is a need to augment, or in some cases replace, the multiple-choice tests with some type of performance assessment. Secondly, several of the multiple-choice tests are not especially congruent with the California curriculum frameworks, and a number of the reviewers felt that they should be replaced and/or supplemented by tests more compatible with the framework emphasis (Wheeler, 1988).

A number of efforts are underway to explore how prospective teachers are assessed for licensure. The California State University system, for example, has undertaken an institutional effort to define the knowledge and skills that prospective teachers need within each subject area. And the California Legislature, in the Bergeson Act (or Teacher Credentialing

Law of 1988) charged the California Commission on Teacher Credentialing (CTC) and the State Department of Education with identifying and evaluating alternative methods of teacher assessment to ascertain whether and how such assessments should be used (potentially in tandem with a beginning teacher support program) in the process of credentialing of future teachers.

This same legislation also established 15 projects providing support to teachers in their first or second year of teaching. The teachers participating in these support projects also agreed to participate in the pilot tests of teacher assessments. The support project, the assessment project, and an evaluation project to determine the efficacy of differing methods of new teacher support together comprise the California New Teacher Project, under the joint supervision of the Commission on Teacher Credentialing and the State Department of Education.

In commissioning the pilot testing of new teacher assessments, the California Legislature has taken the position that although teacher assessments are being used in some other states, most of the existing instruments are unsuitable for use in credentialing California teachers. For example, the Legislature specifically criticized the use of observation instruments consisting of checklists of teacher behaviors. In developing and/or testing a broad variety of new teacher assessments, the Legislature hopes to acquire the information necessary to assemble a package of assessments. These assessments would be given at appropriate stages of the preparation program and early in the teaching career to ensure that every certified teacher in the state of California has the skills necessary to effectively teach students. California has identified and is currently using assessments of a teacher's basic skills (the CBEST) and subject matter competency (NTE Specialty Area tests or, for elementary teachers, the Test of General Knowledge in the NTE Core Battery). While these assessments are aimed at teacher candidates, the Bergeson Act provides for the pilot testing of assessments of teachers in their first or second year of teaching.

The Commission on Teacher Credentialing and the State Department of Education contracted with Far West Laboratory to conduct and appraise the results of the pilot administration of a number of existing innovative measures of teaching. In the following report, we will describe the instruments pilot tested, outline findings from the pilot testing, and provide a summary of our conclusions and implications for the future development of new teacher assessments.

PILOT TESTING

In selecting instruments to be pilot tests, the Commission on Teacher Credentialing and the State Department of Education staff reviewed the literature on teacher assessment and observation and asked national experts and state administrators of teacher assessments to identify instruments that might serve as appropriate prototypes in the pilot project. A large number of instruments, particularly classroom observation systems, were reviewed and found to be inappropriate for pilot testing at this time. A few instruments were identified as promising, because they either employ innovative modes of assessment or they assess significant domains of teacher competence (especially subject-specific pedagogy) that have not been assessed adequately in the past.

The purpose of the pilot tests was to examine how the various assessment components functioned in order to determine whether these assessments would serve as useful models for the state's desired assessment system. Components included such things as prompt materials, scoring criteria, and training exercises for assessors. The assessments were tried out on a small scale, since the focus of the pilot tests was on the functioning of the assessment instruments rather than on the performance of the participants. The ultimate goal of these pilot tests was to find out whether it was advisable to invest additional resources in developing assessments resembling those piloted.

The pilot tests aimed to examine the following:

- The appropriateness of alternative content and modes of assessment

- Identification of the strengths and weaknesses of an instrument in measuring the varied competencies desired of teachers, especially content knowledge, pedagogical knowledge, and pedagogical content knowledge

- The reaction of new teachers to the content and modes of assessment

- Whether and how such assessments could and should be used as future requirements for teacher credentialing

- Fairness across differing teacher characteristics and teaching contexts

- Accommodation of varied teaching styles

- The appropriate stage in a teacher's career to administer requirements for teacher credentialing

- The ability to assess competency to teach diverse students

Assessment Instruments

Six assessment instruments were identified by the Spring 1989 pilot testing: one classroom observation instrument (the Connecticut Competency Instrument or CCI) applicable to all subjects, grades K-12; one materials-based, multiple-choice examination for elementary grades K-8; and four semi-structured interviews. Of the semi-structured interviews, two focused on two different topics in secondary mathematics, one on a secondary social studies topic, and one on an elementary (grades 5-6) mathematics topic.

The elementary mathematics and secondary social studies assessments were developed by Stanford's Teacher Assessment Project (TAP) as part of its prototype test development work for the National Board for Professional Teaching Standards. Both assessments were originally developed for use with master or expert teachers. The other four instruments were developed by the state of Connecticut, or under contract to that state, as part of its developmental work to assess beginning teachers for a professional teaching credential. All instruments were pilot tested, with the exception of the Semi-Structured Interview in Secondary Social Studies, which the two state agencies, Far West Laboratory and the test developer, agreed would require too much revision to make it appropriate for beginning teachers.

The following are brief descriptions of the three types of instruments:

Classroom Observation — Connecticut Competency Instrument (CCI). This is a classroom observation system in which an observer conducts a 45-60 minute observation, focusing on 10 indicators of a teacher's classroom performance. These 10 indicators are grouped in three clusters to represent three major areas of instruction: Management of the Classroom Environment, the Instructional Process, and Student Assessment. In addition to the observation, the CCI system includes a pre-assessment information form that is filled out by the teacher and includes the learning objectives, activities, instructional arrangements, and materials associated with the lesson; a pre-observation interview in which the observer meets with the teacher to go over the aspects of the lesson that the teacher has detailed in the pre-assessment information form; and a post-observation interview in which the teacher meets briefly with the observer to explain any deviations from the plan that may have occurred during the lesson.

A key feature of the CCI, and one that distinguishes it from many other observation systems, is the analysis and rating process. After scripting what takes place in the classroom as accurately as possible, the observer completes a one-page form for each of the ten indicators, writing in one column of the form evidence from the script that supports the indicator, and evidence that does not in another. The observer then weighs the evidence in both columns in order to rate the teacher's performance as either "Acceptable" or "Unacceptable."

Semi-Structured Interviews. These assessments combine two assessment strategies: the semi-structured interview and the assessment center. A semi-structured interview strategy provides opportunities for teachers to respond orally to a standardized series of questions or tasks that are presented verbally by an examiner who uses a script or interview schedule. The interview is semi-structured in that it allows the use of follow-up questions at the discretion of the assessor when a teacher's answer is judged to be incomplete. An assessment center strategy allows for simultaneous assessment of a number of teachers, all of whom participate in a series of exercises or tasks which might otherwise be administered to teachers individually. For these semi-structured interviews, the assessments were organized so that each teacher did a different task in the same time period, rotating through the tasks.

Two Semi-Structured Interviews in Secondary Mathematics (SSI-SM) have been developed by the State of Connecticut as a means to assess the compe-

tency of their beginning teachers of secondary mathematics. The interviews are similarly structured but focus on two different topics: (a) linear equations, and (b) ratio, proportions, and percent. Each interview consists of five tasks:

1. *Structuring a Unit*. A teacher arranges 10 mathematical topics in a sequence appropriate for teaching the unit, explains the reasons based on training and experience, and discusses how the chosen method might affect student learning.

2. *Structuring a Lesson*. A teacher explains how a lesson might be constructed from a topic represented by several pages of a textbook.

3. *Alternative Mathematical Approaches*. A teacher is given alternative solution strategies for a problem, chooses one or more approaches to use in teaching students, justifies the approaches selected, and discusses the relative advantages and disadvantages of each strategy.

4. *Alternative Pedagogical Approaches*. A teacher is shown five alternative curriculum materials, chooses approach(es) to use in teaching students, justifies the approach(es) selected, and discusses the relative advantages and disadvantages of each method.

5. *Evaluating Student Performance*. A teacher is shown samples of student work that contain errors in the solutions, identifies the error(s) made, and offers suggestions about remedial instruction.

The assessment for the Semi-Structured Interview, Elementary Mathematics (SSI-EM) was developed by the Stanford Teacher Assessment Project for assessment of expert teachers. The nature of the tasks varied only slightly, however, from those of the SSI-SM assessment:

1. *Lesson Planning*. A teacher has 30 minutes to plan a lesson on a given topic in mathematics for a 5th grade class, and then responds to questions about that lesson.

2. *Topic Sequencing*. Using a set of 17 cards representing mathematical topics in a unit, a

teacher sorts the cards into groups of topics, selects the cards representing the major themes of the unit, defines the topic on each card, and arranges eight of the cards in order of perceived difficulty for students.

3. *Instructional Vignettes.* A teacher responds to a series of hypothetical situations involving students in after-school tutoring sessions.

4. *Short Cuts.* A teacher is presented with two purported computational shortcuts or rules of thumb for solving mathematical problems and evaluates them in terms of pedagogical and mathematical soundness.

The Semi-Structured Interview, Secondary Social Science assessment is similar in format to the SSI-EM and SSI-SM. The tasks for the assessment are:

1. Reviewing a Textbook
2. Planning a Lesson
3. Use of Documents

Given the level of difficulty of the tasks for beginning teachers and the need for further developments before the assessment would be ready for pilot testing with new teachers, a decision was made to postpone the pilot testing of this assessment.

Multiple-Choice Assessment — Elementary Education Examination. This two-hour assessment was designed for beginning elementary (K-8) teachers, and was developed by IOX Assessment Associates, Inc., for the state of Connecticut. The pilot assessment consisted of six different forms, each with 77 multiple-choice items covering three major competencies: mastery of content knowledge, mastery of knowledge of teaching, and mastery of teaching particular content areas. These items differ from other more traditional multiple-choice items in two respects: 1) The majority of questions are embedded in a classroom situation, e.g., "You are planning a lesson on chemical changes. Which of the following . . . ?"; and 2) Some of the items ask the teacher to analyze reference materials that are commonly used by classroom teachers. These include student worksheets, lesson plans, report cards, and test reports.

Teacher Samples

Far West Laboratory was directed to administer the assessments to appropriate samples of new teachers in the California New Teacher Project and to other new teachers in the state if sufficient samples of project teachers were unavailable. Teacher samples were identified based on their match with the grade level-subject matter of the assessments and their geographic location. All elementary 5th- and 6th-grade project teachers, for example, were identified as potential candidates for the Semi-Structured Interview in Elementary Mathematics (SSI-EM). The final sample for each assessment, however, was determined by the number of potential candidates available in geographically clustered areas. No teachers participated in more than one assessment. The assessments and the sample of teachers for each were as follows:

- Classroom Competency Instrument
    45 teachers
- Elementary Education Examination
    138 teachers
- Semi-Structured Interview-Secondary Math
    (2 assessments)*
    20 teachers
- Semi-Structured Interview- Elementary Math
    41 teachers

Findings from Spring 1989 Assessment Pilot Tests

The above descriptions provide an overview of the different assessment instruments that were examined for use with beginning teachers and the samples of teachers that participated in the pilot testing. In Spring, 1989, Far West Laboratory coordinated the administration of five assessment pilot tests. Upon completion of the pilot tests, we evaluated our experience with each assessment along three dimensions: administration, content, and format (including scoring).

Administration. The ease of administering the assessments varied with the materials-based, multiple-choice examination being the easiest to administer and the semi-structured interviews in an assessment center format (i.e., rotation of teachers and tasks) the most difficult in terms of training for scor-

* Teachers were interviewed in the morning on one topic and in the afternoon on another.

ers, identifying and scheduling facilities and teachers, and conducting the assessment. Based on our experience, we identified the following as improvements needed:

1. Semi-Structured Interview - Elementary Math

    a) Lengthen training for assessors

    b) Redesign tasks so that each consumes approximately the same amount of time

2. Connecticut Competency Instrument

    a) Reduce the number of observations and evaluations to one per day

Most teachers and assessors found the arrangements for the assessments to be reasonable. The two areas of most concern were the timing of the assessments at the end of the school year and the difficulty of the assessors in completing more than one observation per day. Finding the optimal time for assessments seems to be a challenge: teachers were tired after school; during the day they did not want to leave their classrooms and substitutes were not always available; and on weekends teachers often had other commitments, including lesson preparation.

Content. Although analysis of the assessments' congruence with CTC California Standards of Pedagogical Knowledge and Competence for Beginning Teachers and SDE curricular expectations (as defined by the Model Curriculum Guides) will not be available until the end of 1989, we can summarize the teachers' and assessors' perceptions of the content of the assessments.

Teachers generally found the assessments represented by the CCI, the Elementary Education Examination, and the Semi-Structured Interview in Secondary Mathematics (SSI-SM) relevant to the work they perform as teachers. For the SSI-EM, some teachers questioned the appropriateness of the task that required them to sequence topics for instruction. Others questioned the task that asked them to respond to a series of hypothetical situations involving students in after-school tutoring sessions. Teachers felt that the first task was beyond the scope of their work and that the second was "unreal" because it did not provide critical information that teachers use to respond to student questions, such as the student's

temperament, what the student had learned previously, and nonverbal cues from the student during the interaction.

Teachers also differed in the extent to which they felt prepared to perform the tasks required. Most of the teachers observed with the CCI or assessed with the SSI-SM reported feeling well prepared. The issue of lack of preparation surfaced in those assessments specifically geared to elementary teachers. Some teachers who took the Elementary Education Examination or were assessed by the SSI-EM stated that it was unfair to assess a teacher on content that they had not previously taught. This position is especially relevant to elementary teachers because the curriculum differs markedly in content and emphasis between lower-grade (K-3) and upper-grade (4-8) levels. Other teachers criticized the SSI-EM for its lack of recognition that teachers use supplementary materials and resources to assist in instructional design for topics with which they are less familiar. Determining the balance between assessing those subjects and grades covered by a certificate and those in which teachers have taught is a key design issue for which decisions will need to be made concerning credentialing areas and assessment content.

While the SSI-EM and the Elementary Education Examination were perceived as problematic in assessing competency across grade levels, most teachers and assessors thought that the SSI-SM and CCI did a good job in this regard. However, one assessor who observed a vocational education class with the CCI questioned whether this assessment is appropriate for classes where students receive little direct instruction but instead work independently on practicing techniques.

Teachers were asked whether the assessment in which they participated has the capacity to measure a teacher's ability to teach students of diverse academic, cultural, or ethnic backgrounds. None of the assessments was perceived as being completely adequate in this area: The CCI is limited to the range of students in the teacher's classroom; some forms of the Elementary Education Examination (six were pilot tested) did not contain any test items that address teaching bilingual/LEP students; the SSI-SM asked about adapting instruction for the teacher's more or less advanced students, but did not ask the teacher to define the reference group; and the SSI-EM had few questions that focused on either enrichment or remedial instruction.

Format. Teachers were surveyed about the appropriateness of the format of the particular assessment in which they participated. Teachers observed with the CCI tended to view the pre- and post-observation interviews as being especially helpful in allowing them to explain the lesson's objectives and classroom content so that their behaviors were more readily understandable. The change in the format of the materials-based Elementary Education Examination received mixed reviews. (The assessment embeds multiple-choice items in a classroom context, e.g., "You are planning a lesson on chemical changes. Which of the following...?" and asks teachers to respond to items by evaluating materials such as IEPs, report cards, and lesson plans.) Some teachers felt that the items on the new assessment reflected actual teaching tasks more accurately than more traditional multiple-choice test items. Others felt that these items were unable to avoid the limitations of multiple-choice items in that they represented ideal rather than real situations and did not reflect a teacher's knowledge of students and the necessity of making decisions consistent with available resources.

The semi-structured interview format also received mixed reviews. Teachers who participated in the SSI-SM generally liked the format, while those who participated in the SSI-EM were divided. Teachers who viewed their experience favorably generally appreciated the opportunity to talk with another educator about their newly-gained teaching techniques. Teachers who criticized the interview format either preferred to give written responses or found responding to oral questions to be highly stressful. One reason why a greater percentage of teachers preferred the SSI-SM format over the SSI-EM format may be found in the differing purposes of the two instruments. The SSI-SM was designed for beginning teachers, while the SSI-EM was a prototype for identifying experienced exemplary teachers. Thus, the SSI-SM was administered to math specialists and focused on topics that were relatively easy for them, while the SSI-EM was given to subject matter generalists and focused on more difficult topics in elementary mathematics such as fractions, ratios, and proportions.

Because teachers perceived a particular format to have both strengths and weaknesses in critical

areas, there were many recommendations that we use of multiple assessment strategies in order to view teaching from multiple perspectives. In designing and implementing a comprehensive approach to teacher assessment for licensing, the use of multiple formats would be highly desirable. It would capitalize on the strengths of different formats and minimize limitations associated with any particular format.

One format issue that cuts across assessments was feedback. Teachers desired feedback on their performance on the assessments, generally wanting their strengths and weaknesses identified. The majority of teachers elaborating on the feedback form wanted the feedback to occur as soon as possible after the assessment. Appropriate feedback, however, depends largely on scoring results, and of the five assessments administered, only the CCI had a complete scoring rubric. Scoring protocols for the SSI-SM and SSI-EM were still in development, although data should be available late in 1989. Data by subject area on the materials-based Elementary Education Examination will also be available then.

CONCLUSIONS AND IMPLICATIONS FOR FUTURE ASSESSMENTS OF BEGINNING TEACHERS

Although we are still analyzing some of the measures, the following issues have emerged for consideration in conducting future pilots and in developing assessments for beginning teachers.

Purpose of Assessment

California would like the new assessments to serve both a summative and formative purpose. The summative entails insuring that only qualified teachers are granted certificates and that the criteria for granting these certificates represent a sound knowledge and application of teaching content and pedagogy. The formative purpose includes providing information and guidance that will be useful in planning staff development activities and programs to support and improve a new teacher's teaching performance.

Our findings suggest that teachers are very interested in receiving information from the assessments that will enable them to know their strengths and weaknesses. Both teachers and assessors supported the formative purpose of the assessments.

Assessors and some teachers also recognize and support the need to assess more directly the skills and knowledge that are important to effective instruction and to make credentialing decisions based on these assessments. Thus, the summative and credentialing purposes also received some support.

It will be important to consider the tradeoffs and tensions that will exist when an assessment is designed to serve both of these purposes. For example, how a teacher responds in an interview will undoubtedly be affected by whether that response is tied to the granting of certification or even to potential staff development activity. If certification hangs in the balance, they will not be inclined to reveal their areas of uncertainty or weakness. But they may very readily reveal these to obtain support and assistance if the assessment is to serve a formative purpose.

Effect on Preservice/Inservice Programs. Another reason for developing and implementing new assessment systems is to influence the preparation and support given in preservice and inservice programs. Our findings suggest that teachers feel less well prepared to teach math than other subjects in the elementary grades, and are less comfortable with math concepts than secondary teachers with math majors. Also, beginning teachers related that they had much more experience and training in some of the assessment tasks than others. For example, lesson planning was a familiar and relatively easy task as compared to sequencing topics and reflecting on alternative options for teaching. Including these areas and tasks in a credentialing system can have an impact on the attention and support that teacher preparation programs give toward ensuring that prospective teachers have these skills and knowledge. Thus, designing the assessment system to represent the domain of knowledge and skills required for effective teaching and matching these domains to the assessment methods can help lead and shape the preparation and support of teachers.

Scoring Assessments

The lack of scoring systems for the prototype assessments made assessor training difficult and analysis of the instruments problematic. Test developers have been reluctant to develop scoring systems and criteria at an early stage in the development of these types of innovative assessments. The intent of this strategy of development is to avoid limiting or reducing the assessments to that which is easily scoreable and to push the limits of the assessments so that they represent actual teaching skills and competence as strongly as possible. We support this objective, but based on the experience of pilot testing we suggest that scoring systems be developed prior to training assessors and administering an assessment. Scoring criteria and protocols will affect the questions that need to be asked to solicit information from the assessments that matches the targeted areas.

Teacher Samples for Piloting Assessments

Emphasis should be given to creating varied samples of teachers for future assessments. Our experience indicates that increasing the sample size beyond 20 teachers for pilot assessments does not necessarily yield more information data. In particular, assessments might be designed for beginning teachers with different levels of experience (i.e., beginning of first year, end of first year, and so on through the end of the second year) because teachers' knowledge increases markedly from the completion of a teacher preparation program through the second year of teaching. If sample size is increased, teachers from varying teaching contexts should be included. Larger samples of teachers would be more useful at the stage of field testing in which estimates of reliability, comparisons of different subgroups of teachers, etc. were more critical.

Context Issues in Assessment

How can assessments reflect contextual differences in teaching? This question deserves thoughtful consideration as we design assessments. To determine an instrument's capability to competently assess a teacher's ability to teach in diverse contexts, many approaches are possible, but two are obvious: 1) include questions in the assessment about varying instruction for different types of students; and 2) provide specific information about different contexts. Problems identified with some of the questions and tasks used in this study suggest that both approaches to teaching context need further refinement. Also, the interviews and multiple-choice questions are always likely to be limited in their ability to depict teaching contexts well. On the other hand, classroom observations, which are rich in allowing for teaching context, are restricted to the specific context observed. Thus, multiple assessment strategies can help provide different but complementary

TABLE 1

Content of Assessment

1. Does the evaluation or assessment reflect important teaching skills, knowledge and activities? If teachers were to prepare or be prepared to "do well" in the evaluation or assessment, would it likely improve their teaching or instruction?
2. Are there important teaching skills, knowledge and activities that are not included in the assessment?
3. Is the content and pedagogy that is represented or assumed in the assessment consistent with the district's curricular and instructional focus and emphasis?
4. What types of information will be produced? Will the scores or reports be useful for judging and providing feedback on strengths and weaknesses? Will the information yield only a pass/fail decision?

Feasibility of Assessment

5. What are the costs in terms of time and fiscal resources for the assessment, and can the district afford to support these costs?
    a. What initial and ongoing training is needed for the assessors, raters, or judges?
    b. What are costs for the training, for releasing assessors or raters, for supporting teacher time?
6. What level of curriculum content knowledge is required for assessors or evaluators? For example, is the curriculum knowledge that is reflected in the assessment such that a curriculum or content specialist will be needed to conduct the evaluation or assessment?
    a. If special knowledge is needed, e.g., math expertise to judge or evaluate teachers' ability to teach math, is there a pool of potential assessors within the district or nearby with this knowledge?

Reliability of Assessment

7. Is there information to support the reliability or consistency of the assessment across:
    a. occasions
    b. raters or judges?

approaches for incorporating and assessing teachers' ability to adjust and teach in different contexts.

Implications for Local Assessment Decisions

We have described some of the options that are being explored to move teacher assessments away from checklist approaches, tests of basic skills, and indirect measures of teaching toward more authentic forms of assessments. It is possible that districts and local agencies may want to consider alternative approaches or at least review their evaluation systems in light of this movement. We outline some questions that might be useful guides in reviewing and deciding on teacher assessment or evaluation systems in Table 1.

These are not presented as a complete set of criteria. They are illustrations of questions that should be asked when considering alternative teacher assessment or evaluation purposes.

SUMMARY

The above represent findings from our early examination of alternative forms for assessing beginning teachers. It appears that assessments that more authentically represent the knowledge and skills required for teaching have promise. If that promise is realized, these types of assessments can help shape the support and instruction provided to beginning teachers, clarify the domains that are critical for teachers and that can be incorporated into credentialing or other assessments, and increase the public confidence in the quality of the teaching force.

California's future plans include developing and pilot testing alternative forms of teacher assessments, designing a system that will combine the complementary features of these different assessment forms or modes, and developing alternative forms of teacher support systems. These activities can help to achieve the promise mentioned above.

REFERENCES

Boyer, E.L. (1983). *High school: A report to the Carnegie Foundation for the advancement of teaching.* New York: Harper & Row.

Goodlad, J.I. (1984). *A place called school: Prospects for the future.* New York: McGraw-Hill.

Holmes Group, Inc. (1986). *Tomorrow's teachers: A report of The Holmes Group.* East Lansing, MI: The Holmes Group.

National Commission on Excellence in Education. (1983). *A nation at risk: The imperative for educational reform.*

Shulman, L. S., & Sykes, G. (1986). *A national board for teaching? In search of a bold standard.* A report for the Task Force on Teaching as a Profession. New York: Carnegie Corporation.

Wheeler, P., Hirabayashi, J. B., Maretinson, J., & Watkins, R. W. (1988). *A study on the appropriateness of fifteen NTE specialty area tests for use in credentialing in the state of California.* Emeryville, CA: Educational Testing Service.

Wheeler, P. & Elias, P. (1983). *California Basic Educational Skills Test: Field test and validity study report.* Berkeley, CA: Educational Testing Service.

Wise, A., Darling-Hammond, L., Berry, B., & Klein, S.P. (1987). *Licensing teachers: Design for a teacher profession.* Santa Monica, CA: The Rand Corporation.

CONCLUSIONS

Insights
and Principles

Ann I. Morey
Mary Gendernalik Cooper
San Diego State University

I N the opening chapter, the major forces influencing recent initiatives to provide support and assistance to new teachers were discussed. That chapter also provided an advanced-organizer of the topical issues examined in subsequent chapters. This concluding chapter provides a synthesis of insights gleaned from the conceptual and experiential reflections of the contributing authors. We close by recommending some guiding principles for both new teacher assistance program development and for framing on-going policy considerations.

PROGRAM INSIGHTS

Chapters 3 through 6 explore in considerable depth distinct dimensions of new teacher support programs. Together they provide a coherent framework for developing such programs; a framework sufficiently flexible to accommodate diversity in implementation. These chapters also contribute to understanding the content of the California programs in terms of two pervasive characteristics — informed responsiveness and the evolving nature of the programs. Content is determined and shaped by the experience and expertise of program staff and the new teachers themselves. Content encompasses issues related to personal well-being as well as professional skills and understandings. Content evolution is reflected in the expansion of topics from year to year and in the ways in which topics are linked and sequenced. The San Diego State University/San Diego Unified School District Retention Program, for example, addressed classroom discipline issues as the highest priority topic in its first year. By the second year, insights and reflection led project staff to address discipline in conjunction with motivation; in the third year this content dimension evolved further to engage the new teachers in considering how their instructional repertoire as well as their motivating strategies were influencing classroom discipline. This example suggests one of many kinds of evolutions which take place in the treatment of content in programs for new teachers. Evolutions occur as a number of forces and factors interact. Their specific character will depend, in part, on the guiding conceptions of the program, as well as program staff's interpretations of program experiences and program impact data. They also will depend on program staff efforts to integrate other sources of insight, such as relevant research, into their program reviews and revisions. Lastly, the programs will be influenced by the deepening nature of the collaboration itself as the partners increase their knowledge of each other's strengths and resources and further develop their working relationships.

The program elaboration chapters clearly suggest a more integrative model of support and assistance than that represented by Mitchell and Hough's typology. Their typology is useful to analyzing the relative emphasis of different components within an actual program. Most of the extant programs weave together elements of professional acculturation (standards of practice and professional identity) with elements of acclimating to the immediate school, district and work-group context. This is accomplished through such program dimensions as the organizing strategies (e.g. clusters, content or site-based group meetings), project staff roles, and the treatment of content. There may be variability of emphasis across programs on these dimensions, but virtually all of the programs encompass them.

The chapters which explore program dimensions further suggest that substantial benefits accrue to district-based staff development/inservice programs, university-based preservice programs, and to program staff as well as to the new teachers and their students. Chapter 6 suggests that there are distinct learnings and insights to be gained from working with and in support of beginning practitioners which enrich individual professionals as well as other program areas for which they have responsibilities.

COLLABORATION

Besides providing a comprehensive understanding of support program elements and effects, the central chapters of this book suggest a great deal about the quality and character of collaborative work. Collaboration among professionals in support of new teachers is both institutional and personal. It provides opportunities for understanding the institutionally distinct purposes and tasks, the bases for structural arrangement, the norms of practice and the language of the institutional culture. As much as we are all in the same business, collaboration among school districts, universities, and teacher's associations makes us aware of how differently we may perceive and approach that business. Collaboration allows us to learn about and from each other. And, as in the case of new teacher support programs, creatively combine each other's expertise in pursuit of shared purpose.

Collaboration can be a means to correcting misconceptions and distrust which ignorance built. It can be a powerful vehicle for new arrangements and alternative resource allocations. Through collaborative programs such as the new teacher support programs, university faculty maintain better contact with the world of practice and this informs their judgments in designing or revising preservice programs. Similarly, collaboration affords experienced teachers a means to keep abreast of research and innovative models of practice and to contribute to these endeavors. Collaboration is a way to acknowledge and incorporate, through an expanded period of preparation and induction, the ever expanding knowledge base of pedagogy. It communicates a powerful image that learning to teach is a life-long collegial venture. Further, it enhances integration and articulation of theory and practice through a guided period of transition from student to professional practitioner, not unlike other professions.

Collaboration can promote and help sustain institutional as well as personal renewal. It is, nonetheless, taxing, time-consuming, sometimes intrusive. On the basis of the programs reported herein, the benefits of collaboration make the effort worthwhile. All of these programs are in some sense collaborations, involving various combinations of the seven key groups of players identified by Mitchell and Hough. It should further be noted that 80 percent of the original *California New Teacher Project* proposals were school-district/university collaboratives. There is undoubtedly a broadly-based perception that such arrangements are mutually beneficial.

CONCEPTIONS AND ASSESSMENT

It is evident from the discussion in Chapter 9 regarding the assessment initiatives for teacher credentialing and licensure that the guiding conceptions of teaching and teacher are not those embedded in more prevalent *performance-observation-for-detecting-specific-behaviors* assessment models. The developing assessment protocol reflects a deeper understanding of the complexities of teaching and teacher thinking. The assessments are being designed to reveal and probe teachers' decisionmaking and the content and pedagogical knowledge which undergird and give meaning to the overt deliberate actions of teaching.

Standards and assessments related to teacher licensure must be recognized as categorically distinct from support and assistance initiatives. The two enterprises need not and ought not be discordant. To the extent that both efforts emanate from congruent conceptions of teacher and teaching and are grounded in the same theoretical and research paradigm they can symbiotically support each other. Together they can serve as powerful catalysts for exemplary professional practice and on-going professional growth. To the extent that structures and networks can be made to facilitate continuous communication between these

two efforts, they will enrich and inform each other, to the ultimate benefit of the teaching profession as a whole, and to the students of California's public schools.

Laura Wagner opened this book by describing the characteristic diversity of California's population, politics, and public education institutions. In education, at least, that diversity can be woven into a resilient cloth only if there are informed comprehensive conceptions of who we are, what we are about, and the goals we are pursuing. Diversity, then, becomes a well-spring from which ideas, models, strategies and approaches for deliberate action are forged. Within this framework, delegations of authority and responsibility are not used to separate interests or perspectives, nor to create counter-productive status hierarchies.

CONCLUDING THOUGHTS

We began this book by examining how the current interest in programs for new teachers stems from a concern for the quality of public education in the United States and from increased recognition of the many challenges new teachers face. The impending teacher shortage and the staggering statistics regarding the proportion of new teachers who leave the classroom during their first five years of teaching have added to the impetus for such programs. The initial evaluations of the California programs indicate that these programs are successful in assisting novices to become professional educators. The data also suggest a dramatic increase in the retention of these teachers. Clearly, the programs are having their intended impacts.

We conclude with some general observations. Teaching is a complex task involving an extended period of preparation and a lifelong journey involving continuous professional development. In addition, today's teachers face special challenges related to the increasing ethnic and linguistic diversity of students, the changing societal context and the condition of public education. Programs to assist new teachers must be based on conceptualizations which recognize this complexity and which provide a organizing framework for the actual program. In current practice, the presence and influence of different frameworks is sometimes more tacit; embedded in specific activities rather than clearly articulated and serving as the guiding standard for determining assistance efforts. We maintain that programs will be more coherent and effective if the relationship between the operational program and the conceptual framework is more explicit.

Such conceptualizations will lead program organizers to move away from providing assistance at just the survival level. This was most obvious in the California case by the move from first year program emphasis on classroom management and discipline to increased focus on motivating students, instructional performance and professional development.

Our experience has lead us to focus also on the importance of the selection and preparation of the individuals who provide assistance. Relatedly, the benefits to the providers in terms of their own professional growth and in the execution of their responsibilities have been impressive.

We are convinced that whenever possible collaborative models of assistance should be implemented. The combined expertise and other resources of the collaborating partners produce a more effective model of assistance. As public policy is formed regarding new teacher programs, we believe that the nature of these collaborations should be defined in very general terms. Matters regarding who the collaborators are and fiscal agents should be decided by local groups. Our experience with the fine models designed and implemented in this diverse state have led us to this conclusion. Further, we are impressed with the amount of in-kind resources and "volunteered" extra time that has been contributed to the projects. We are concerned about the ability of institutions and individuals to sustain such efforts over the long term. Given this situation and the large public investment in preparing a new teacher, we hope that California will not be penny wise and pound foolish in its decision regarding what constitutes sufficient resource support for programs for new teachers.

The California experience is just one of many efforts to assist new teachers occurring throughout the country. We are impressed simultaneously by the similarities and diversity across our programs and believe our experience is not unique to our state. We have tried to capture our knowledge about providing assistance for the development of new teachers, and in the process have discovered that we have grown as professionals through our work with them and with our colleagues in the schools, teacher associations, universities and state level agencies. We are encouraged by the dedication and growth of the new teachers as we know that the youth in our schools will benefit from their efforts.

APPENDIX A

Resources

Carol Withers
San Diego State University

CONFERENCES AND WORKSHOPS

Association for Supervision and Curriculum Development National Training Center Summer Program
(A variety of 5-day programs)
Association for Supervision and Curriculum Development
125 N. West Street
Alexandria, VA 22314-2798
(703) 549-9110

Case Approach to Mentor Training
Judith H. Shulman
Far West Laboratory
1855 Folsom Street
San Francisco, CA 94103
(415) 565-3000

Effective Instruction and Instructional Management
(Three workshops: Effective Instruction; Effective Supervision; Planning/Monitoring of Staff Development)
Michele Garside, Coordinator
San Diego County Office of Education
6401 Linda Vista Road Room 405
San Diego, CA 92111

Three workshops: class management, raising student productivity, instant involvement seminars
Meredith Fellows
5865 Friars Road, # 3405
San Diego, CA 92110

Language Development Across the Curriculum Training Modules
Charles S. Terrell
San Bernardino County
Superintendent of Schools
601 North E Street
San Bernardino, CA 92410
(714) 387-3135

PRIVATE TRAINERS

Management teaching tools
Rick Morris
4305 Gesner Street, Suite 202
San Diego, CA 92117
(619) 276-6301

Geraldine Flaherty
Peer Coach Trainer
Performance Learning Systems
224 Church
Nevada City, CA 95959
(916) 265-6264

Positive Parent Relationships Training
Lee Canter and Associates
P.O. Box 2113
Santa Monica, CA 94087
(800) 262-4347

Randy Sprick
Teaching Strategies, Inc.
P.O. Box 5205
Eugene, OR 97405
(800) 323-8819

Training Workshops (a variety of topics)
Karen Olsen
California Institute for School Improvement
1107 9th Street, Suite # 150
Sacramento, CA 95814
(916) 447-2474

Bonnie Williamson
Dynamic Teaching Company
P. O. Box 276711
Sacramento, CA 95827
(916) 638-1136

For Bilingual and English as a Second Language contact:
The California Association of Bilingual Educators
926 J Street, Suite 810
Sacramento, CA 95814
(916) 447-3986

BOOKS AND HANDBOOKS

Association for Supervision and Curriculum Development Supervision Library
(A variety of books)
Association for Supervision and Curriculum Development
125 N. West Street
Alexandria VA 22314-2798
(703) 549-9110

Attracting, Retaining, and Developing Quality Teachers in Small Schools
(cite order number RL-9040-588-WR)
The Regional Laboratory for Educational Improvement of the Northeast and Islands
290 South Main Street
Andover, MA 01810

Beginning Teachers and Professional Development
(cite order number PPD-706-10882-WR)
Central Regional Educational Laboratory
295 Emroy Ave.
Elmhurst, IL 60126

Bright Ideas by Meredith Fellows
(160 ideas to involve students in productive thinking)
Meredith Fellows
Box 81
Fallbrook, CA 92028

The Holmes Group Forum (free)
The Holmes Group
501 Erickson Hall
Michigan State University
East Lansing, MI 48824-1023
(517) 353-3874

Mentor Handbook
Northwest Regional Education Laboratory
Marketing Office
101 S. W. Main Street
Portland, OR 97204

The Mentor Teacher Role: Owners' Manual by Karen Olsen (1987)
Karen Olsen
California Institute for School Improvement
1107 9th Street, Suite 150
Sacramento, CA 95814
(916) 447-2474

Crossing the Schoolhouse Border by Laurie Olsen
California Tomorrow
849 South Broadway, Suite 831
Los Angeles, CA 90014
(213) 623-6231

Preparing Mentors for Work with Beginning Teachers: A Leader's Guide to Mentor Training
Publications
Far West Laboratory
1855 Folsom Street
San Francisco, CA 94103
(415) 565-3000
or
ERIC Clearinghouse on Educational Management
University of Oregon, Eugene
1787 Agate Street
Eugene, OR 97403-5207

Knowledge Base for the Beginning Teacher by Maynard Reynolds (editor)
Pergamon Press
Maxwell House, Fairview Park
Elmsford, NY 100523
(914) 592-7700

The Intern Teacher Casebook by Judith H. Shulman and Joel A. Colbert (1988)
Publications
Far West Laboratory
1855 Folsom Street
San Francisco, CA 94103
(415) 565-3000

The Mentor Teacher Casebook by Judith H. Shulman and Joel A. Colbert (1987)
Publications
Far West Laboratory
1855 Folsom Street
San Francisco, CA 94103
(415) 565-3000

Sourcebook for Rural Educators by BethAnn Berliner
Publications
Far West Laboratory
1855 Folsom Street
San Francisco, CA 94103
(415) 565-3000

The Solution Book byRandy Sprick
Teaching Strategies, Inc.
P.O. Box 5205
Eugene, OR 97405
(800) 323-8819

Teacher Preparation for Rural Schools
(cite order number NL-788-WR)
Northwest Regional Education Laboratory
Document Reproduction Service
101 S. W. Main Street, Suite 500
Portland, OR 97204

A First-Year Teacher's Guidebook for Success by
Bonnie Williamson
Dynamic Teaching Company
P. O. Box 276711
Sacramento, CA 95827
(916) 638-1136

For Bilingual and English as a Second Language, contact:
David Dolson, Assistant Manager
Bilingual Education Unit
California State Department of Education
721 Capitol Mall
Sacramento, CA 95814

VIDEOS

Another Set of Eyes
Part One: Techniques for Classroom Observation (over 90 minutes, 80 page trainer's manual)
Part Two: Conferencing Skills (over 120 minutes, 80 page trainer's manual; available for purchase, rent, or preview)
Association for Supervision and Curriculum Development
125 N. West Street
Alexandria, VA 22314-2798
(703) 549-9110

Classroom Episodes
(A set of ten videos, may be purchased separately; available for purchase, rent, or preview)
Association for Supervision and Curriculum Development
125 N. West Street
Alexandria, VA 22314-2798
(703) 549-9110

Classroom Management with Pat Wolfe
Association for Supervision and Curriculum Development
125 N. West Street
Alexandria, VA 22314-2798
(703) 549-9110

How You Can Be a Super Successful Teacher (an audiotape)
Dr. Harry Wong
1536 Queens Town Ct.
Sunnyvale, CA 94087

Management teaching tools
Rick Morris
4305 Gesner Street, Suite 202
San Diego, CA 92117
(619) 276-6301

Randy Sprick
Teaching Strategies, Inc.
P.O. Box 5205
Eugene, OR 97405
(800) 323-8819

For Bilingual and English as a Second Language Curriculum, contact:
Tim Allen, Director
Second Language Division
San Diego City Schools
4100 Normal Street
San Diego, CA, 92103-2682
(619) 293-8096

APPENDIX B

Contributors

T HE editors would like to express appreciation to participants at the invitational workshop on Beginning Teacher Programs and the Bay Area Regional Planning Seminar on Supporting New Teachers and others who have contributed to this guidebook.

Allen, Lana
Milpitas Unified School District

Balch, Pamela
San Diego State University

Barloga, Mary Beth
San Leandro Unified School District

Berg, Marlowe
San Diego State University

Bernhardt, Victoria
California State University, Chico

Berry, Jan
Modesto City School District

Bevilaqua, Louise
John Swett Unified School District

Bissell, Joan
University of California, Irvine

Blackney, Denise
Upland Unified School District

Brinlee, Pat
Commission on Teacher Credentialing

Brown, Jim
San Francisco State University

Bye, Tom
Vallejo City Unified

Cates, Carolyn
Far West Laboratory

Cauchi, Paul
Milpitas Unified School District

Chryst, Sue
Pittsburg, California

Colvin, Carolyn
San Diego State University

Cooper, Mary Gendernalik
San Diego State University

Cooper-Shoup, Susan
California State University, San Bernardino

Cronenwett, Susan
Sacramento City Unified School District

Dawson, Donna
San Jose Unified School District

Dianda, Marcella
Southwest Regional Laboratory

Ely, Evelyn
E. M. Cox School

Fitch, Phil
Commission on Teacher Credentialing

Folsom, Roxie
Burlingame School District

Gair, Stefan
Pittsburg Unified School District

Garmston, Susan
State Department of Education

Getridge, Carolyn
Oakland Unified School District

Ginelli, Frank
Gilroy Unified School District

Ginwright, Sylvia
La Mesa/Spring Valley School District

Godbold, Delores
Roosevelt Junior High School

Green, Jennie Spencer
California State University, Chancellor's Office

Harris, Cynthia
California State University, Hayward

Hightower, Cheryl
Alameda County Office of Education

Hogan, Kathy
San Mateo Schools

Holtzmann, Jane
California State Department of Education

Hoover, Mary Lee
Livermore Valley Unified School District

Hope, Donna
New Haven School District

Hopper, Mary
San Diego City Schools

Hough, David
University of California, Riverside

Hunter, Ena I.
Pittsburg Unified School District

Hunter, Jim
Berryessa Union School District

Johnson, Yvonne
Cajon Valley Unified School District

Johnston, Fabiola
Los Angeles Unified School District

Kapic, Linda
Lodi Unified School District

Keitel, Christine
Cajon Valley Unified School District

Kelly, Pat
United States
International University

Kohonen, Viljo
University of California,
Santa Cruz

Krahenbuhl, Janice
Gilroy Unified School
District

Lass, Mary Jo
California State University,
Long Beach

Lemoyne, Frances
San Mateo Unified School
District

Loucks, Sharon
Fresno County Office of
Education

Mackie, B. J.
Cabrillo Unified School
District

Majetic, Dick
Commission on Teacher
Credentialing

Martin, Nancy
California State University,
San Bernardino

McBride, Susan
California Polytechnic
State University,
San Luis Obispo

McClung, R.E.
Centralia School District

McLevie, John
Commission on Teacher
Credentialing

Merseth, Katherine K.
University of California,
Riverside

Miller, Ernestine
Claremont Middle School

Mitchell, Douglas E.
University of California,
Riverside

Mitchell, Jim
Santa Clara Unified
School District

Moran, Marilyn
Sequoia High School

Morey, Ann I.
San Diego State University

Muniz, Sophia
Fresno Unified School
District

Murphy, Diane
San Diego State University

Myatt, Keith
Burbank Unified School
District

Nagel, Anne
San Diego State University

Nielsen, Donald
California State University,
Los Angeles

Perotti, Paul
Milpitas Unified School
District

Raczka, Don
Poway Unified School
District

Ratzlaff, Charlotte
San Mateo Union High
School District

Riggs, Iris
California State University,
San Bernardino

Ritchie, Lorraine
San Leandro Unified
School District

Roberts, Michael
Winters Joint Unified
School District

Roth, Rob
California State University,
Long Beach

Sandlin, Ruth
California State University,
San Bernardino

Shaw, Bev
Milpitas Unified School
District

Shulman, Judith H.
Far West Laboratory

Sleiman, Vicki
Poway School District

Sly, Carolie
Alameda County Office of
Education

Sweetland, Greta
Upland Unified School
District

Swihart, Virginia
New Haven Unified

Todd, Larry
Orchard School District

Towner, Arthurlene
California State University,
Hayward

Van Wyke, Carol
Upland Unified School
District

Wagner, Laura
State Department of
Education

Ward, Beatrice
Southwest Regional
Laboratory

Warren, Betsy
Berryessa Union School
District

Wasserman, Susan
California State University,
Northridge

Waters, Louise
California State University,
Hayward

Watson, Maria
California State University,
Hayward

Weir, Cathy
San Mateo City Schools

Wierman, Starla
Winters Joint Unified
School District

Wiggins, Lorna
John Swett Unified School
District

Wilkins, Jan
San Jose Unified School
District

Williams, Diana
Long Beach Unified
School District

Williamson, Sandy
Alameda County Office of
Education

Withers, Carol
San Diego State University

Worthy, Regina
San Francisco Parkside
Center

Wright, David
Commission on Teacher
Credentialing

Yanos, Mary Ann
Walnut Valley Unified
School District